CW00487247

# THE DREAM MIND

**WILLIAM J. NAUGHTON** (Bill) was born in Ballyhaunis, Co. Mayo in 1910 and lived for many years with his wife Erna on the Isle of Man, where he died in 1992. The film based on his novel *Alfie* became one of the classic films of the sixties. Bill Naughton was also a noted playright, with plays such as *Spring and Port Wine*, and he also wrote short stories, children's books and three celebrated volumes of autobiography.

# THE DREAM MIND

*How and Why We Dream*

William J. Naughton

ARCADIA BOOKS

Arcadia Books Ltd
15–16 Nassau Street
London W1W 7AB

www.arcadiabooks.co.uk

First published by Arcadia Books 2009
Copyright © Erna Naughton 2009

William J. Naughton has asserted his moral right to be identified as the author of this work
in accordance with the Copyright, Designs and Patents Act, 1988.

All rights reserved. No part of this publication may be reproduced in any form or by any
means without the written permission of the publishers.

A catalogue record for this book is available from the British Library.

ISBN 978-1-906413-32-3

Typeset in Garamond by MacGuru Ltd
Printed in Finland by WS Bookwell

Arcadia Books gratefully acknowledges the financial support of
Arts Council England.

Arcadia Books supports English PEN, the fellowship of writers who work together
to promote literature and its understanding. English PEN upholds writers' freedoms
in Britain and around the world, challenging political and cultural limits on free
expression. To find out more, visit www.englishpen.org or contact
English PEN, 6–8 Amwell Street, London ECIR IUQ

*Arcadia Books distributors are as follows*:

*in the UK and elsewhere in Europe*:
Turnaround Publishers Services
Unit 3, Olympia Trading Estate
Coburg Road
London N22 6TZ

*in the US and Canada*:
Independent Publishers Group
814 N. Franklin Street
Chicago, IL 60610

*in Australia*:
Tower Books
PO Box 213
Brookvale, NSW 2100

*in New Zealand*:
Addenda
PO Box 78224
Grey Lynn
Auckland

*in South Africa*:
Quartet Sales and Marketing
PO Box 1218
Northcliffe
Johannesburg 2115

Arcadia Books is the *Sunday Times* Small Publisher of the Year 2002/03

*'I have not fished in other men's waters.'*

John Bunyan


*'We must be grateful to God that He created the world in such a way that everything simple is true and everything complicated is untrue.'*

Gregor Skovorada
Eighteenth-century Ukranian philosopher

# Contents

1 The Function of Dreaming                        1

2 Scientific Sidelights                          15

3 Sexuality in Dreams                            23

4 Guilt in Dreams                                31

5 Arousal Dreams                                 39

6 Wish Fulfilment or Fobbing Off?                47

7 Recall – Research – Retribution                55

8 Dream Impulsion                                61

9 Symbols and Sovereigns                         69

10 Hypnosis and Dreaming                         75

11 The Disparate Twins                           81

12 Extrasensory Perception                       85

13 Visual Stratagems                             91

14 The Dead in Dreams                            99

15 Dream Stimuli                                107

16 Daily Dream Drama                            113

17 Idiosyncratic Dreams                         117

18 Moral Pointers in Dreams                     129

19 Writing and Dreaming                         139

20 Films, Plays and Opera                       147

21 Lunch Dream – Lucid Dream                    159

Commentary                                      167

# 1

# *The Function of Dreaming*

The key to an understanding of all dream phenomena lies in knowing how we actually dream and why. Once that is grasped the enigma of sleep and dreaming largely explains itself, and dreaming can be seen for what it is – a biological safeguard of the sleeping person (and of all mammalian life). Freud and Jung were both aware of this possibility, Freud at one time declaring dreams to be 'the GUARDIANS of sleep' (his capitals); later, alas, he was to dismiss sleep as a 'physiological problem'. Jung made a most acute observation on what is the basic nature of dreaming: 'One does not dream, one is dreamed.' Also: 'It is on the whole probable that we will continually dream, but consciousness makes while waking such a noise that we don't hear it.' William Wundt (1832–1920), the founder of experimental psychology, regarded dreaming as a study for physiology – certainly not the preserve of psychiatry that it has become – and maintained that sensory stimuli inspired our dreams; he was also convinced that the explanation of the sleep-dream phenomenon would be an unambiguous one, which indeed it is. The function of dreaming being almost totally understood, the study of sleep has become a mishmash of speculation.

Dreaming and sleep are – despite all impressions they may leave to the contrary – a dual function, invariably concurrent. They start together – there can be no sleep without the dream's protective monitoring – they proceed in perfect unison, synchronised and interdependent, their mutual correlation so absolute that they are virtually the one state. The moment the dream is cut off we awaken. Dreaming provides a vital link with our senses as we lie vulnerable during sleep, with apparent sight and hearing being excited from dormancy by a flow of imaginary episodes, a sensory impression of touch is activated by contact with sheet or skin; taste and smell require an actual stimulus to function fully. The impression of a dream following a planned scenario is an illusion; although a continuing theme or situation is set up to engross the dreamer, the development of the dream must remain open-ended, ready to diverge at any moment to accommodate the exigencies of sleep. Sound and movement need to be simulated and absorbed into the dream happenings, as well as various physiological stimuli, such as thirst or hunger, penile stirrings, indigestion and much else. If these were not assimilated by the dream flow our sleep would be continually broken. Even more importantly, should we be safer awake – for example, mucus in the throat, a threat to an infant or the elderly – we can be aroused by a dream shock. Sleep, therefore, is not a random state of total insensibility – hazardous to primitive man in his cave, and even precarious to us in our beds – but a governed state of unconsciousness.

At night when we switch off the light and lie down in bed, vague fancies tend to cross the mind, and if we are tired and in need of sleep we usually begin to yawn, with reverie of one kind or another taking over as reason gives way to delusions without our realising it. (Should we be excited, however, or anxious or worried, to a degree that these feelings are too intractable to be absorbed into a dream, then we remain awake until they have abated, and the need for sleep becomes more compelling.) Almost nothing of this early period can be recollected; to observe it one needs to keep an alert gleam of thought alive, then at the final moment force oneself to escape the pervading grip of sleep, sit up and write down what was going on in one's mind. I have done it frequently – although it is not a practice I recommend, as it can cause disorientation – and have been taken aback to discover that what I had assumed to be rational thought turned out to be pure fantasy. Incoherent utterances often break out during this state, there is a slump of the body, known as the 'hypna-gogic jerk', and at the onset of sleep it would appear that the 'stream of consciousness' is taken over by the Dream Mind – the name I have given to the agency that converts this unceas-ing, efferent mental flow into dreaming. Jung's observation on our being 'dreamed' is now realised, for dreaming is a most tightly controlled phenomenon. There is just the necessary glimmer of consciousness during sleep to involve us in the dream happenings and to react to them, but not enough to question their reality (without some degree of consciousness during sleep we could not of course remember any of our dreams). This serves a further purpose in that mental activity is never entirely cut off, ensuring a quick revival of our senses on awakening. I have summarised here what took me many years to comprehend, and I do not expect the reader to grasp it fully from a single reading, so different is the function of dreaming from received opinion, and notions we have been fed from childhood. However, most of this theory should be simple to validate in a sleep clinic.

If we dream continually throughout sleep this must pose questions about certain established dream theories, among them that of REM and Non-REM sleep. I shall simplify for the sake of clarity: NREM sleep occurs on average over three-quarters of our sleep, with REM sleep, rapid-eye-movement sleep, a quarter, in alternating cycles of some ninety minutes of all sleep. Sleep research appeared to indicate that most dreaming occurred during REM sleep; and although REM sleep had the spiky EEG pattern of light sleep, the sleeper's musculature was relaxed, the arousal threshold high, which are signs of deep sleep; because of such contradictions REM sleep became known as D sleep – desynchronised sleep or 'paradoxical sleep', and NREM as 'orthodox sleep'.

A more likely explanation of the REM phenomenon, I would suggest, is without any paradox. There are three phases preceding REM sleep, by which time sleep is at its deepest, a state when the sleeper would be most difficult to arouse by dream shock, which means he is most vulnerable, consequently it is expedient to intensify dreaming to keep a firm control. This dream excitation stimulates neural activity, causing higher pulse and respiration rates, and increased blood pressure. Dream happenings are now at a dramatic pitch – probably the reason for the rapid eye movement – which means simultaneous attempts at arousal by external means will be ineffective because of the tighter hold of the dream.

Various other characteristics of REM have puzzled researchers, such as why in the early sleep period REM should be absent. The reason would appear to be that the sleeper is not at risk during this stage – had he been then sleep would have been inhibited at the start. Why, it has also been asked, do infants have proportionately much longer periods of REM sleep? An infant is much more vulnerable during sleep, the mortality rate is alarmingly high, so that infants are in more urgent need of the safeguard of vivid REM dreaming to ensure that dream arousal is not delayed. No sleeping baby should be so tightly wrapped that there is a restraint on the convulsive limb jerkings that facilitate awakening; nor should any child that has been given a 'soothing medicine' be left unattended. The frequent nightmares of childhood are probably extreme arousal devices demanded by children's deep sleep. (I am confident that were an electric blanket placed under the sheet of a subject in a sleep clinic, and switched on high during a NREM period, that REM manifestations would result, and soon the person would be aroused, and able to recall his dream.)

There is a further REM teaser; why is it that the echidna, *Tachyglossus aculeatus*, the spiny anteater should of all viviparous animals – those bringing forth the young in a live state – be the sole exception to REM sleep? The spiny anteater is one of the Monotremata, an order of the most primitive mammals, and native of Australia and Tasmania; it inhabits scrubland, is solitary and elusive, rarely observed outside captivity, in which it has been known to live for fifty years. The adult is eighteen inches long, has strong poisoned claws and sharp spines; when threatened it can roll itself into a spiny ball or dig itself into soil or disappear under a crevice. It lives mainly on ants, can fast for a month, and arouse itself at any time from hibernation; it also has a significantly large neocortex, indicating high intelligence. Is it possible that the spiny anteater has such inherent all-round protection that it remains invulnerable during sleep – the only mammal that can dispense with the safeguard of dreaming?

Keeping in mind the intrinsic unity of dreaming and sleep, various other fallacies about dreaming can be confuted. The 'dream within a dream' phenomenon, for instance, has given rise to the most involved explanation, when the actual reason is simple and obvious. Nothing happens in a dream that is without purpose, and a vital requirement in successful dreaming – some dreams are perfect and others are makeshift – is the dreamer's total belief in the reality of all that happens to him, whether flying unaided or having his head cut off. The demand of the dream in presenting a train of instantaneous images, however, which must keep to an apparently plausible sequence, not unlike that of a film, results in an occasional slip-up. It needs only a moment of wakefulness, causing a hiatus in the dream flow, to let in an extra speck of consciousness, and with it an intrusion of reason. During the writing down of my own dreams, I have often marked a juncture at which a suspicion had arisen in my mind as to whether the events were real or only a dream. At once, as credence wavered, it would be intimated to me that yes, it was only a dream – or on occasion that it was a play or film I was watching, or a book I was reading. Sleep continues, but the grip of the Dream Mind on the dreamer is weakened, the secondary sensation of onlooker being less intense than that of protagonist, therefore it is necessary that the dreamer be caught up in the hyper-reality of the normal dream state as soon as possible, which demands further manipulation to get back on course.

Flying and falling dreams have attracted varied speculation, which surprises me since they are so obviously arousal dreams. Flying dreams I have had often, they usually occur at a volatile period, or those of exceptional fitness; when I used to jog almost daily I had many flying dreams. Sometimes they serve for getting the dreamer out of a difficult situation, should he be threatened. In one such dream I found myself in the City of London, being hailed by stockbrokers, and as I wished to get away, the idea was prompted to me: You can fly in your dreams – why not try it in real life! With that I took a deep breath, gave a spring upward, levitated uncertainly, then by hand movements as though I had wings, I rose up between the tall buildings, waved to the astonished City men, and was away. The sensation of flying and falling dreams evokes a preparedness in the dreamer for alighting on the ground, and this is significant in that it avoids the confused state of mind that follows on any abrupt awakening: the sleeper is braced for action – either to run or to repulse.

Lucid dreams are another misunderstood phenomenon. Figuratively, they may be said to arise from a disharmony between Hypnos, the god of sleep, and his son, Morpheus, the god of dreams, with neither prepared to let go his grip on the sleeper. There is a notion that because the dreamer knows he is dreaming, and has the illusion of volition and reasoning, he can do as he wishes. This is far from so, the dreamer has no choice in what he will do, but is prompted in his actions without being aware of it, and no matter how much he may be able to think *he cannot think himself awake*. In every one of my own lucid dreams I have followed what I took to be my reasoning, the consequence of which has led to a shock arousal – which must have been anticipated by the Dream Mind. In one such dream I found myself in a railway station, a throng of passengers hurrying past me, one a man on stilts. I get into my compartment, assuring myself that it is all a dream, and that in fact I am secure in my quiet bed at home fast asleep, and to confirm my belief – and this is a frequent prompting – I decide to take hold of the tweed coat of the passenger next to me, and give it a tug. At once he turns on me, much annoyed, and I apologise profusely. That I find to be the most disconcerting aspect of the lucid dream, the discovery that every object and person the dreamer takes for illusions turns out to be only too real.

At this point it may be pertinent to explain how I, a layman and amateur dream researcher, whose only laboratory has been his bedroom, can write with such conviction about dreaming and sleep – refuting most of the accepted theories on the subject. For some forty years I have made a practice of sitting up in bed on awakening and writing down dreams, which asks for aptitude and training, as it needs only one extraneous thought to banish a dream from mind. Insomnia has been an aid – the sleeper who gets a regular seven hours will have difficulty recalling any dreams. This recording of dreams was for no other purpose than their inclusion in a journal I kept, for although I had read Freud and Jung I remained unpersuaded about the contrasting theories of dream interpretation. On occasion, however, I must admit to having used dreams in my writing – one made a good scene in *Alfie*, a play-film I wrote; and in 1973, a BBC radio play of mine, based on one of my own dreams, was awarded the Prix Italia. It was that same year, on Tuesday, November 27th, that I found myself awake around two o'clock, my sleep having been disturbed by the sound of an airplane overhead, the fading drone of which I could still hear, with the final scene of a dream vividly in mind.

*Dream*: I am standing in a queue at a bus stop outside Selfridge's on Oxford Street, waiting for a 73 bus. A number of other buses go by and finally I look towards Marble Arch and spot the 73 bus coming along. What comes chugging up to the stop is not a bus but an old-fashioned American train, one recalled from films, although I am not aware of any incongruity. I feel a flurry of excitement as I clamber up the high external steps, wait for the other to enter, then put my foot through the open doorway, at which crucial moment the scene vanishes and I find myself awake.

I decided that the dream did not merit being written down, and as I lay there alone in the darkness a thought crossed my mind: I was within a fraction of entering the train compartment, *What would it have been like inside?* The scene must have been set in my imagination, I reasoned, and as the daily task of writing had developed skills in tracing elusive ideas and fancies, I let myself become absorbed by the tail-end of the dream once more, hoping to catch a vestige of the image ahead. I tried again and again, but failed completely, all I encountered was nullity, a blank void. There's something strange about that sudden end, I think, as I give up the search and rest back. Then suddenly the answer presented itself: *There had been nothing ahead!*

That, I deduced, meant that dreaming and sleep proceed synchronously, neither one getting ahead of the other. I was already inclined to believe from my own experience that we probably dream throughout sleep – but I wasn't yet convinced of it. I switched on the bedside lamp, got up and wrote the surmise down in my journal, taking it to be nothing more than an item of interest about dreaming, and that that would be the end of the matter. Yet by a chance in a million I had struck upon the 'open sesame' to an understanding of all dream phenomena – the intrinsic concurrency of dreaming and sleep, their being one indivisible function. That indeed is the fundamental point I wish to make. I had no desire to study dreaming, it just happened that night after night, as I was writing down a dream, some new insight would reveal itself. I merely served as an amanuensis – the faithful slave always on hand to write down what he was prompted. The sheer fascination of coming to an understanding of various dream phenomena kept me going nicely (the transformation of bus into a hissing locomotive for instance, was a device to simulate the crescendo as the plane flew over the house, and also to involve me more in the dream, the train being a more exciting image than a bus, in an effort to sustain sleep, which just failed). Over the following years a most comprehensive theory evolved as many hundreds of notes accumulated, these were conflated into successive manuscripts as new insights were revealed. A capacity to unfold elusive imagery, and perceive obscure stimuli, that developed over my years of writing, was a decided help. Dreaming is an endless study – faces and places lose their impact when repeated too often and need replacement. I have exhausted numerous characters, various dream situations that once engaged or scared me.

Dream theory has become riddled with misconceptions – sexuality in dreams, symbols, the dead, guilt in dreams. Guilt, by the way, is such an essential factor in creating our dreams, that it is often dream-hatched from some imaginary dream wrongdoing, that may serve better than the real thing, since it is only hinted at, and remains murky and obscure, difficult to trace to source. This concoction will burden the credulous dreamer with a sense of guilt, one that will ferment the dream brew. For this reason alone, psychotherapy based on dream interpretation tends to seed itself in the patient's psyche, and become self-perpetuating. Nothing that happens in a dream, I must emphasise, need affect the conscience of the dreamer, be it rape, incest or murder – its only purpose being sleep-related. Unless one enjoys dreams for their sheer novelty, or is an artist who can get the occasional insight from them, I feel it may be as well to accord with the amnestic nature of dreaming and forget one's dreams completely: 'Do not spread compost upon the weeds to make them ranker.' I prefer to forget my own by writing them at once in a journal; since psychotherapy is an area of which I have had no personal experience I shall say no more, and instead of rebutting further sophisms I will end with a recent dream.

After lunch I was about to rest when a friend telephoned to ask me about Soho of forty years ago; then as I was going to my bedroom I let in our neighbour's cat, which we were looking after, and as I did the thought struck me that it was much better behaved than any of our own four cats. I was thinking I might mention this to my wife, but as she is not one to go in for too much training, I decided not to – possibly she is right, I thought as I got into bed, maybe we impose our wills too rigidly on our pets. With these impressions in mind I fell asleep, and this is how they were dream-resolved.

*Dream*: I am walking through Soho with an old friend called John when a playful collie dog comes prancing up to us. Being fond of dogs I stoop to stroke it, which it likes, and I make a fuss of it generally. Then remembering that John doesn't care for dogs, I tone down the play, and raise a commanding finger, 'Sit!' I tell it, 'Sit!' The dog wants to play, not sit, but seeing that I am insistent it sits for a moment and then goes bounding off. John and I continue our stroll, and further on at a corner we see the dog again, and I beckon to it, and stoop to greet it: 'No, thanks!' the dog calls out to me, 'I want no more of that! Why, you've no sooner made friends with me than you start giving orders, "Sit! Sit!" and all the rest of it.' I feel much ashamed, and apologise to the dog, 'I'm awfully sorry,' I say, 'you are perfectly right. I ought not to have made you sit down –' The dog, however, does not wait to hear me out but scampers off, leaving my words in the air. I find that John is no longer with me, and I go off on my own, thinking over the incident. Presently I see a school out of which boys are hurrying, and among them is one boy that I recognise as being the collie dog. This pleases me, for now I feel I can make my apology in full, and I begin to smile and greet him as he draws near, but he has already seen me, and as I approach him he calls out 'Pooh! Pooh!' and goes off leaving me standing there.

I woke up feeling much chastened. And thinking how the Dream Mind absorbed my mental impressions, spinning them out into such an episode, fusing the past and the present, a catharsis of sorts, one which gripped me throughout my half-hour sleep, I took this intelligence not to be the Unconscious so much as the Superconscious.

## 2

# *Scientific Sidelights*

Among the proliferation of books on dreaming was one that caught my interest, *The Dreaming Brain* by Allan Hobson (Basic Books, 1988). Hobson, Professor of Psychiatry at Harvard Medical School, and Director of a laboratory of neurophysiology, gives a comprehensive description of the neurobiological activity of dreaming. Unlike most dream-research authors, he puts in certain of his own dreams; above all he is excellent in his account of the neuron, the spider-like nerve cell, with its nucleus, appendages of nerve fibres – axons which carry nerve impulses from the cell body, and dendrites which carry information to it, also the connecting synapses, which transmit impulses from one cell to another. '...*If we assume that each of the twenty billion cells...has ten thousand...communicative contacts, or synapses, then the actual number looks something like this: 200,000,000,000.*'

This explains the simplicity of instant dream presentation; there is no delving down into the past, since every memory from infancy to old age is available, as fresh as can be, for in dreams the time is always the immediate present. It would seem to me that those millions of neurons are grouped according to the various impressions made on the dreamer throughout life – fear, anxiety, sexuality, shame, humiliation and countless others. It needs only one to be tapped, such as that of sex, and a cluster of others from infancy onward are excited, and an erection during sleep will set going a vivid flow of libidinous scenes in which the dreamer is utterly involved. Although the heat is kept up, fulfilment is withheld – that would arouse the sleeper – until finally he wakes up and goes to the toilet to urinate, at which the entire sexual pantomime will evaporate.

Hobson writes: 'We begin by asking the most general and – we think – the most fundamental questions about dreams: Where do they come from? Why are they so strange? Why are they so hard to remember? And what purpose do they serve?' Dreams, I would deduce, spring from a primordial mental zone unaffected by thought or reason – that of all mammals. They are formed out of the countless impressions we have absorbed, more so the recent preoccupations, and reflect the dreamer's own capacity of imagination ('What is Imagination,' said James Joyce, 'but Memory'). There are examples of poets dreaming poems, composers melodies, artists pictures, and more than one scientist has told of how an idea came to him in a dream; indeed, a plumber has told me of his nights being racked by dreams of mislaid wrenches and gaskets that don't fit. Dreaming is at once the most complex yet clear-cut operation imaginable, a marvellous synthesis of varied and contrasting phenomena, of instincts and desires; it seems incredible how all these, in their varying pressures, can be fused into a single dream flow.

*Why are they so strange?* Dreams are strange only in the way drama, poetry and fiction are often strange – the more strange and compelling the more they exercise the imagination, and thereby override reason. Is *Oedipus Rex* or *Hamlet* strange, or science fiction? Equating dreaming with reality is totally misconceived – a more apt comparison would be that of a dream and a movie; the criterion being that you are held by it *as it is happening in your imagination* (no matter what you may later feel). The motivation of every dream lies in the key emotion by which it is charged – reason and commonsense play no part, nor are they intended to. To mention a few dream inconsistencies of my own – I have seen huge battleships sail around Piccadilly Circus, ocean liners go down the Vauxhall Bridge Road, I have glided along Oxford Street one Saturday afternoon in Concorde. One may ask why, and the answer is, dream expediency; the various mental images were at hand, and in their bizarre conjunction engrossed the imagination.

*Why are they [dreams] hard to remember?* is another Hobson question. Dreams are hard to remember because it is proper to their purpose that they be quickly forgotten, as retention would disorganise our later dream life. Recurring dreams and themes would not work, since threats which become familiar but are never carried out, soon fail to instil fear – and fear is what provokes arousal. *What purpose do they serve?* That, I take it, I have answered. *Why, for example,* he asks, *do the powers of reasoning and memory decline in our dreams?* They do not decline so much as that they are inhibited – a necessary measure. The dreamer, when he is flying among the clouds, is allowed a primitive form of reasoning: It must be reality because it is happening to me! Another poser he raises is: *How are we able to perceive visual images in our dreams?* I am convinced that dreaming is analogous to a motion picture being imposed upon the imagination of the dreamer in a sequence of swiftly moving frames – although only once over all those years have I detected such a device. (I imagined it was a unique insight of my own – one which I was even hesitant about putting forward – only to learn later that the Roman poet, Lucretius, had anticipated me by some 2000 years. Although this astonished me, I felt immensely flattered to find myself apparently alone, in this respect at least, in the company of that great humanitarian philosopher. No man could be closer to my heart than one who had the courage to throw scorn on the religious ideas of his day, those of death, judgement and damnation. The bus in my own dream did not simply transform itself into a train, what happened was that one set of frames replaced another; the train interior would have demanded new frames (possibly that was the crucial point at which I awoke). Often in a dream we enter our present home to find ourselves in our childhood home – by a sequence of new frames. The correspondence between film-making and dreaming is seen in various aspects of the dream: the long shot, medium shot, the close-up, also the black-and-white dream and the coloured, and the attempt at novelty and suspense – but never the dream comedy.

Dream impulsion is of various kinds, there is the purely visual artifice – I saw a sailor having his head blown off in a naval battle, then replaced by another sailor, after which they started chatting. (Decapitation is a common dream device – a dramatic happening to the dreamer, simple to perform.) There are dreams of which the pith is sensation, such as flying and falling dreams, of gliding and skating, evoked by a certain psycho-physiological state. Tactile impressions can be perfectly simulated in a dream – the sleeper's hand on a silk pyjama creating a feeling of caressing a female thigh, of resting on his hairy chest that of the pubic area. Dreams arising from hunger or thirst have a basic dissimilarity from the former – no illusion of eating can satisfy hunger, nor any amount of dream water assuage thirst, although they may try to feign such. Neither can the sense of smell – a more vital faculty than is commonly imagined – be evoked in a dream; the olfactory receptors, sensitive and myriad in number, are situated in the mucous membrane at the top of the nasal air passages, and can be excited only by a real smell, not an imaginary one.

Hobson, however, can enjoy the appetising smells he misses in his dreams, and even the gustatory titillation of wine – should he so wish. Arrangements should be made that when he is deep in sleep, a pan of fried bacon and onions, or similar savoury dish, is set beside the bed, and the lid removed. This sensory intrusion of sleep must be absorbed, and no matter what the dream situation happens to be, piquant aromas will season it. He can even be made to taste dream wine by having his lips dabbed with a Burgundy during sleep. All this I know from my own dream experiences, but it can be confirmed by the famous researchers, Maury and Hervy de Saint-Denis, both of whom Hobson mentions. Among other questions that exercise his curiosity is that of why pain should be so unusual in dreams, considering certain scenarios in which one would expect it. A dream, to work – that means to keep a tight control on the dreamer's imaginational reactions, so that sleep can be preserved, yet arousal swiftly realised – must grip the dreamer to the exclusion of all else. Pain in a dream would exert a diversionary pull, creating a situation which the dreamer would tend to resist. The only dreamer who is likely to have pain-motivated dreams is a masochist. Pain is of course present in dreams when the dreamer has some actual pain, toothache or a sore finger – which will then be drama-tised, such as in the extraction of all the teeth or amputa-tion of the finger. This inflated presentation overshadows the actual sensation of pain, absorbs it, and ensures sleep.

Hobson also points out: '…dreaming often mimics mania and a panic anxiety state but rarely depression.' Depression is the converse of mania and panic anxiety, in that it is a lowering of the vital powers, a sinking down, a state wholly lacking dyna-mism. (Note that dream drama rises as the dream progresses.) The more depressed a person is, the greater need in his dream life for dream drive of a panic or anxiety source, to keep the dream on the move. Nor will cheerfulness serve the purpose of the dream, because high spirits dissipate and cannot support a long dream. A person who goes to bed depressed will not have a cheerful dream, because the dream would not take off; our dreams must fit our moods. It may have been noticed that laughter is rare in dreams; the reason being that laughter is a response that dispels, and as such would terminate a dream. Fear and apprehension, which can be aroused in a moment, are the most potent dream motivators.

Hobson devotes much space to the dreams of the 'Engine

Man'; this is a manuscript he acquired, a dream journal, of a bachelor aged forty-six, who lived with his mother and two sisters, had several romances but never married. In 1939 he recorded, within the space of three months, 233 dreams, varying in length from one to seventy-eight lines, together with dream drawings. Hobson, who brings REM into his analysis, makes what I take to be a false distinction between 'hallucinoid dreams' and 'thought-like activity occurring in sleep' – if one is thinking during sleep I take that to be dreaming. He also goes into much probing about why the Engine Man should describe in detail the colour of suits, apples, faces and much else he saw in dreams.

I was much impressed by the quality of the Engine Man's recording of his dreams; 233 dreams written in three months indicates the unceasing nature of dreaming, since these would represent only the dreams recalled on awakening. Nor should we ignore the extreme likelihood that he had other dreams, possibly of a sexual nature, which he was too discreet to put into writing. The various descriptions of colour in the dreams are natural in one who is an artist. Finally, my assumption would be that the Engine Man was a railway enthusiast. (This is something of a craze, and thousands of railway buffs come every summer to the Isle of Man where I live, to ride on the old-fashioned steam trains, which are a tourist attraction.) I would wager that not only did he go to work on a steam train daily, but that he lived close to a railway track on which trains went by at night; his dreams being an expression of preoccupation with trains, and a sure way of representing in dreams the noises of the night.

# 3

## *Sexuality in Dreams*

Lecherous dreams, especially those of a perverted nature, have been said to indicate inclinations in the dreamer of a like nature, or at best an unconscious predilection towards the same. This is a mistaken inference. It need hardly be said, however, that anyone who cherishes deviant desires, indulges fantasies of them, but is careful never to reveal himself, is much more likely to dream of them than is someone who never gives them a thought. Any feeling, sexual or not, which is intimate, secret and suppressed, will animate dreams. Sexuality and dreaming, cognate as they are, born of the same primitive womb, collude naturally – morality or willpower cannot hope to prevail against such a compulsive pair. A penile stirring during sleep, often the tumescence resulting from a full bladder, would detract from the dreamer's rapt involvement in the dream happenings, so there must be a swift absorption of such a stimulus into the dream flow. This can only been done by giving sexual expression to it in dream form. These episodes are usually of such a voluptuous nature that no real life experience could ever match them (such salacious dreams are unlikely to occur, or at least to continue for long, in the conjugal bed). An illicit element often adds spice to the happenings, the situation having had to be tacked on to the dream. I dreamt of being at Wembley Stadium with my wife at the Cup Final, for example. We are up in two corner-seats in the back row watching the football match, with thousand of spectators around us, when I become aware of a sexual urge. A murky veil of mist hangs over the stadium, and taking advantage of this my wife and I are soon engaged in the most improper antics, whilst all about us the crows are yelling away. Suddenly the darkness lifts and I am struck with alarm at what we are up to in front of thousands. The shock awakened me. I got out of bed, went to the toilet, and all lewd desire left me.

Significance is often given to some form of sexual intimacy taking place in a dream between the dreamer and a close relative; since it is essential that we dream without pause, the image of almost any person who turns up instantly will serve. Even a passing recollection of someone before going to sleep, in a context devoid of sexual feeling, will leave an impression on the mind; during sleep, should penile erection occur, the asexual impression may become attached to it, the dreamer finding himself or herself engaged in erotic play with a person towards whom he or she has never had such feelings. The imagination is capricious, and in our daily life, even on solemn occasions, certain fancies and notions of a trivial nature flit across the mind. In dreaming similar darting ideas may intrude, which cannot be shed once they have produced a dream character, and the character has to be found a role. Such intruders are often quietly forgotten once they have served a purpose. A character may turn up in a dream because he or she reminds us of someone once dear or detested, then in the course of dreaming may become associated with a nocturnal sexual excitation, or there may be erotic fantasies brought on by a high temperature. To dream often of a person there needs to be or have been a certain tension in the relationship – apprehension, misgiving, admiration, dislike, love, envy or fear, which may have had to be concealed, as happens frequently between a child and an exacting parent; the image of a dominant character makes a lasting impression. We do not dream of those who fail, one way or another, to engage, annoy, upset or impress us. A prerequisite for any character turning up in a dream is the ready availability of the image; these are often the ones with whom we have lived under the roof, such as parents and siblings.

Regression – the taking up again of an earlier phase of life – is a common ploy in dreaming. In which case, the self of the dream being that of the period, incestuous imagery may easily be evoked, and should such dreams prove effective they will be repeated, and may become a theme for recurring dreams. There could be an indication here of the reason for Freud's emphasis on juvenile sexuality, and his assumption that most neuroses stem from suppressed feelings of that nature. The most tense and difficult sexual phase for the male is often that of boyhood or adolescence; the suppression of desires and the secrecy demanded produce a pocket of feeling that will motivate many an adult dream. Boyhood sexual urges remain especially potent in that they remain unfulfilled, unlike those of a later period, which may often be wiped from memory by an orgasm. Sexual feeling unrealised perpetuates itself in an unsatisfied longing; the same appears to be true of love denied consummation – it remains alive for that very reason.

Dreaming, although it plays on the moral susceptibilities of the dreamer, is common to all the class of *Mammalia*, it antedates civilisation, and as such it would seem reasonable to assume that it is amoral. Consanguinity, I am convinced, is unapprehended by the Dream Mind – the only significant factor being the impact a character may have on the dreamer. One's mother or father in dreams, one's children, brothers and sisters, are individuals devoid of any ties of kinship, the familiarity or intimacy the result of having been brought up together – as occurs in the animal world. Peculiar partners in dreams need not surprise us, when we consider the inappropriate roles certain persons we know play in non-sexual dream situation – a surgeon operated me in one dream and when he took off his mask I saw it was a coal-filler I used to know. Any juxtaposition, no matter how grotesque, is possible in a dream, providing it serves the immediate need of keeping the dream moving. Good and bad are neutral concepts in dreaming, as is meaning – these have to do with a civilised intelligence, the dream plays solely on feelings.

Since it is not in nature for any human being to escape carnal desire, this when suppressed becomes intensified, bursting to get out, in the way some grudge we felt in early life may rankle over the years. Covert or stifled feeling does not expire, and during sleep may produce a night of dreaming. No one need ever be the least troubled in conscience for any action performed in a dream, any more than for something read in a newspaper or book or seen in a film. To put it simply – the dreamer can be made perform acts in his dreams which in waking life would be repugnant to him or her; we are responsible for our behaviour, but not for the often wild and violent fancies that cross the mind.

The sexual element in dreaming is often incidental, the real determinant being the inhibition it gives rise to. Therefore, *moral* repression is not the reason obscene sexual acts are manifested in dreams, but repression itself. There is no end to the imaginary defects over which persons suffer obsessions, from that of shame about humble beginnings to concern about the shape of ears, nose or the lack of hair – which secret worry makes good emotive dream stuff. The more a person talks about his inhibitions or sexual fantasies, the more liberated he becomes from them, and the less prone he is to dream about them. Luis Buñuel, in his autobiography *My Lost Life*, speaks of what he discovered rather late in life, the perfect innocence of the imagination: 'I say, "All right, I sleep with my mother, so what?" and almost immediately the image of crime and incest depart, driven off by my indifference.' The lesson would seem to be, shed our conscience as you go to sleep. After that didactic outburst here is a dream of my own with a sexual motif – of a kind I regard not as erotic so much as entertaining.

*Dream*: I am living in our ground floor flat in St George's Square, and there is a keen sense of the place, of the house being fairly crowded, with people living in rooms beside and above us. I happen to go into the next flat, where there lives a young Chinese woman, and also a small boy, and find myself in the bedroom (which in the dream has become the back bedroom of our home in Bolton where I lived as a boy). I chat away to this young Chinese woman, who is shy, polite and very nice, and the next thing, much to my surprise, I have talked her into letting me get into bed with her. The boy is still in the bedroom in his own bed but doesn't know what is going on, since he has gone to sleep, and anyway I gather that he is innocent about sex. (This situation in an echo of one from many years earlier, of a woman who invited me to her home, but who had a small son, whose sleeping presence in the home utterly inhibited any sexual urge I might have had.) The Chinese girl is warm and pliant, for it seems I am in a persuasive mood, and her simple innocence engages me, so that soon we are about to make love in what seems to be a felicitous coming together. Voices are suddenly heard on the landing outside, and I gather there is a survey going on about noise. (How do I know there's a survey about noise, since I haven't heard their actual words? This is one of the dreaming peculiarities which neither Freud nor Jung mentions: the explanation is that in dreaming there is much intimated without being aware of such. Often we have no reason to know of circumstances or indeed to recognise characters – situations and identities having been suggested rather than observed.)

Next, by the same means, I gather that the people at the door are two young women and a man from the flat below my own, and they start knocking loudly on this bedroom door. (Every situation and happening in the dream mirrors something similar in my life.) I don't know what to do, for I think to myself, if they see me, the seemingly respectable Mr Naughton, in bed with this girl, it will make a proper scandal. (This is another example of the Dream Mind evoking a much younger self in dreams.) I whisper to this Chinese girl to get up quickly, go to the door, lock it or keep them out, but instead she stays in bed beside me. The next moment the door is pushed open and these three come in to start enquiring about noise. Before they see me I pull the blankets up, cover my head, leaving only my bare feet showing; at least, I tell myself, they won't be able to recognise me by my feet. They start asking the Chinese girl questions, and I am aware that they can see my form in bed, and I imagine they are looking at it, so I wonder to myself how can I change my normal voice so that they won't recognise me, and take me for someone else. In a flash I have the cunning idea to pretend to be a Chinese man – reasoning to myself that this might be a likely possibility. After a little silent rehearsal under the blankets, with the interrupters talking away and asking questions, I manage to strike what I take to be a high-pitched Chinese voice, and start roaring out as if in a temper: 'Feek off! Feek off!'

This tactic proves successful, and almost at once the party go off. I am much pleased at this turn of events, but realise that next they will go to our flat, and the fact that I am not there may create suspicion. I now have to explain to the girl in bed beside me that I must get up, that I have to get back to our flat without the party of my wife discovering me. I feel ashamed at having had to pretend to be Chinese, and in my excitement in having put such a vulgar expression on the lips of an assumed countryman of hers, and above all have qualms about cutting short such a promising liaison. She seems quietly understanding, and I creep off, feeling myself to be a bit of a slob, at the same time regretful that I haven't taken her telephone number. I manage to get back into our flat undetected (it turns out to be not our flat, but the front kitchen of my childhood home in Bolton). I find I can talk to my wife without giving myself away, but we have a visitor, a onetime schoolmate, whom I haven't seen for forty years. I have to stifle my greeting, as I can now hear the trio outside the door, and am afraid that if I open my mouth some betraying echo of the Chinese voice might escape. So I go up to him and whisper anything I have to say. I can see he finds my behaviour rather odd. Next I awake to find I have slipped down in bed and I am very warm. I will not go in further explanation of the dream, but so vivid and real was the experience of it, and so closely did it mimic real life, that when I woke up I first treated it as reality, and only after seconds did I realise it had been a dream. I might add that although I wrote down this dream at once after awakening, and did so as faithfully as possible, I am not unaware of the fact that any recountal of a dream is lacking the intensity of feeling and sensation experienced by the dreamer.

# 4

## *Guilt in Dreams*

Murder and most crimes are relatively rare among people at large, but a feeling of having been involved in something of the kind is common in dreams. One reason for this is that the imagination from the earliest age is fed with stories of menace and violence – as anyone who has read the Bible will know – and in adult life the news media report daily on felonies of every kind. Homicide appears to be such an absorbing subject that numerous plays and films are set around it, and there is an endless spate of fiction devoted to the hunt for the killer. It would be strange indeed if some of this mayhem did not lodge in the mind. And from that source are our dreams fabricated and dramatised – from anything the imagination has been exposed to. I emphasise that it may or may not have a moral reference to the dreamer. In our dreams we have no choice, and must behave as we are induced to behave, although this may be remote from our personal standards, and often contrary to our natural propensities, but after such dreams we are left with a sense of guilt. Such feelings should be firmly dismissed, in the knowledge that our dream corruption was all part of a performance put on to safeguard sleep.

What dreams do reflect is not the character of the dreamer but the temperament, and a person inclined to despondency cannot escape depressing dreams – neurosis and dreams make snug bedfellows. 'I have hardly had any but terrible dreams for thirteen years,' wrote the poet, William Cowper. 'They have either tinged my mind with melancholy or filled it with terrors... If we swallow arsenic we must be poisoned, as he who dreams as I have done must be troubled.' St Augustine tells how there remained in his memory 'the images of such things as my ill custom had there fixed', and after his conversion he had such sensual dreams 'that these false visions persuade me unto that when I am asleep, which true visions cannot do when I am awake. Am I not myself at that time, I Lord my God?' he asked, 'Is my reason closed up together with mine eyes? Is it lulled asleep with the senses of my body?' That wise man was sane enough to conclude that for his dream deviations he was not responsible.

Philosophers and poets have touched upon the subject of guilt in dreams, but I should like to point out what is a more insidious aspect of guilt and dreaming. First, how does the guilt motive operate in dream? How can a person wholly innocent of such notions of fantasies in daily life be made dream of having committed theft, arson, incest or even murder? It should be understood that every night of our lives in the pursuit of sleep, each one of us is exposed to the potential blackmail of a power which is aware of our every deed, word, thought and feeling since birth. By confronting us with hidden feelings that betray so much that we had forgotten, and of which we would prefer not to be reminded, the Dream Mind can hardly fail to grip our immediate attention – its sole purpose in dreaming. It is cunning at playing up any mania or phobia of the dreamer, exploiting any fear, suspicion or jealousy, evoking memory of any moral lapse, and by dream drama intensifying the feelings. It is not, as has been postulated, that suppressed feelings surface in our dreams so much as that they provide the essential nucleus of emotion to charge them.

The dreamer vaguely imagines the dream self to be his present self, but in fact he is totally subject to former feelings, those of childhood or adolescent. Should a person have ever dreamt of being involved in any shameful act, let alone committed one, then that dream incident, the anxiety it gives rise to, together with other dream experiences of a like nature, become closeted in a memory bank, the contents of which in time assume a vague reality. By frequent recurring dreams on the same motif a kind of psychic osmosis is produced, in which the emotive fantasy of the dream filters through the screen of conscious awareness, inducing in the dreamer a waking dread or fear, vague and irrational, but one no less telling.

Guilt of some kind or other seems ingrained in human nature, and almost no one escapes some blot or other, often stemming from a trifle, but magnified by introspection. A mind free of guilt lacks the yeast to set going the dream brew, and even the most austere ascetics, no matter how they avoid sin during the day, must submit to the nocturnal misconduct of their dreams. 'Shut out the whole world, and all the throng of sins;' wrote Thomas à Kempis, 'sit thou as it were a sparrow alone upon the house-top, and think over thy transgressions in the bitterness of thy soul.' Such a keen compunction in such a saintly man would indicate a guilt generated by dreaming, from an uneasy seed of conscience. A loving mother who has lost a child will often blame herself, parents tend to censure themselves for delinquency in their children, many a grown-up person regrets not having been more understanding of parents. In the dreams of such ones a sense of guilt will quickly take root, and serve as a theme of innumerable dreams. Sleep being so essential to life, the most monstrous but meaningless dreams will be inflicted in pursuit of it. And so intense is the dream experience that even the most intelligent minds seem incapable of making a sharp distinction between reality and dreaming – a function that has a clear teleological explanation.

An example from my own vault of guilt dreams is one that used to recur often, setting me back in London, together with an old mate I used to meet in the West End. He lived by his wits, gambling and touting tickets, and there was a shifty air about him, which by our intimate chats appeared to rub off on to me. In my dreams there would arise a recurring situation in which my mate and I have at some time in the past been jointly guilty of murder, a dreaded secret which we share, and over which he is inclined to use a bit of blackmail on me – he having less to lose than myself should our crime be discovered. In these dreams no actual mention of the crime is made, but ominous hints are dropped, and in time my sense of guilt grew – one of complicity in murder. The dreams occurred in what was probably the most guiltless time of my life, yet there was this accumulation of stifled remorse and fear, so that the repeated impact of the dream grew stronger. For some time it may have been that I preferred to dodge the issue, push such thoughts aside, and during my daydreaming periods harboured guilt feelings.

One morning I woke up after a dream in which it was whispered around that I know something about a man killed by a lorry some months before, over whose death there is a mystery, which the police are investigating. In my mind is the guilty thought that a mate of mine, working with me, fixed the so-called accident, and that I am somehow involved in it. But when I talk to my workmates making out I know nothing about the man's death, I feel guilty, and am thinking to myself: You reply just like a guilty man would – try to think how an innocent man would reply. All the time I feel guilty, but am hoping to prove myself innocent – and am longing that one day it will all be forgotten and that perhaps I can shed my feeling of guilt. I even wonder ought I go to the police and 'confess' – although what to confess I am not sure.

After waking up I lay there in bed feeling curiously depressed, but after a time, the dream fresh in my mind, I decided to tackle the issue, and began to ask myself what had I done to draw upon myself such a lump of guilt. Suddenly as I was going over the dream the whole thing became clear: the dreams, I realised, had engendered their own particular feelings of guilt, concocted over the years. This perceptive moment was an absolute liberation – I couldn't imagine how I had let myself be deluded for so long, marvelled at the cunning of the Dream Mind, and felt a sense of total relief. Then it struck me that in my dreams I have been guilty of arson, of seeing rows of small houses burning away, and somehow I am the guilty one – although I have never given arson a thought, except that in recent years I have enjoyed making garden bonfires.

Guilt is only one of a number of feelings upon which the Dream Mind will play; envy, jealousy, distrust are others, and above all any suspicions a husband, wife or lover may have about his or her partner. Those persons who have the least reason to worry are often those who worry most; this lack of stress must be made good, and to this end the Dream Mind will plant some seed of suspicion and intensify it. Sexual jealousy and suspicions of infidelity will intensify, particularly in those who spend much time alone, are often idle, and can dwell upon them; being unspoken such feelings make the most intoxicating dream activators, creating vivid impressions that linger in the mind. As for guilt itself, the more susceptible a person is to prompting of conscience, the less likely he is to commit that act the thought of which disturbs him, but the more often such an act will come up in his dreams. That certain feeling which has been stifled in waking life has acquired a dynamic urge thereby, which would have expired had it been let out – and possibly been spoken about. Similarly, those who most fear muggings, burglaries and crime generally, are usually the ones who find news and talk about such most gripping.

Psychotherapy could be most effective in divorcing the

imagined from the real – in getting the patient to see that certain dreams do not enlighten our doubts or our guilt, but instil them. On the other hand, the dreamer might rid himself of the guilt residue of all such dreams, simply by getting up, making tea, thinking over the dream, taking it right back to its source, seeing the fabrication for what it was – a trick played on him. This convincing oneself of one's innocence deflates further guilt dreams and they soon cease.

Among certain primitive peoples dreams were often regarded as omens, some good and some bad, and were much mulled over, especially so among American Indian tribes, who were not rushed in their way of life. We should appreciate that among illiterate peoples, and the uneducated, the personal and human note figures much more in their social exchanges, and they are more in touch with and guided by that primal intelligence in which dreaming has its source. Not only are they more intuitive, and sensitive to dream intimations, but are not without adopting their own safeguards in this respect.

For instance, I read that in certain primitive cultures they have devised the following method for getting rid of 'bad' dreams. The dreamer gets a suitable lump of clay, takes himself off to a secluded spot, and there he sets up the clay clod in front of him, and tells his dream to it – possibly a form of confession. Then having exorcised it and all its evil portents, he breaks up the clay and crushes it into tiny fragments, disperses them to the wind, and thus gets rid of all influence and possibly memory of his dream. This is similar to the advice given by the anonymous author of *The Cloud of Unknowing*, a fourteenth-century mystical work of singular force and eloquence, in which the writer advises aspirants to the contemplative life to shed all remorse – which, he explains, will only hinder them in their search for God – by gathering all memory of their sins together, putting the lot in a bag and flinging it away. In the absence of a good spade and the chance to work up a sweat digging a garden, I can think of no better alleviation of anxiety, unless it is a five-mile jog. As the great Meister Eckhart tells us: 'Sins truly repented, which God has forgotten, 'tis no business of ours to remember.'

5

## *Arousal Dreams*

It is recognised practice in play constructions that should a shooting or poisoning occur in the last act some passing reference to the gun or poison will be made in the first act; the reason being that such a dramatic happening would fail in its purpose were it sprung upon a wholly unprepared audience. The Dream Mind, so far as is possible, prepares the dreamer for arousal, which ensures that he does not wake up disoriented and confused. Every dreamer has his own particular dream situation to which he reacts with a sense of foreboding, followed by fear, panic and finally shock. Most recurring dreams are arousal dreams; if they were not it is unlikely we would recall them so clearly – the dream we remember being the last one of the series. 'If it works' goes the theatre adage, 'leave it alone.' This is true of the mother telling the same bedtime story to a child, and it is clearly true of dreaming. Once the Dream Mind has hit upon the motif that succeeds it will repeat it until it is worn out. Falling and flying dreams are probably the most common arousal dreams, but they are of an infinite variety.

A woman told me of a recurring dream she used to have

when she was a girl: 'I was about twelve at the time, and I must have had it for what seemed like three or four years. I'd be coming downstairs from my bedroom, and there was a narrow passage at the bottom leading to the living room, and on my left there was an alcove with shelves, where my mother had little ornaments. Now just as I was approaching this narrow part I used to get nervous, because a hand would suddenly come out – stretching towards me. It wasn't a man's hand, or an ugly hand, but a pale, clean woman's hand; it would reach out at me and frighten me. Now it seemed that by luck I always had a hairbrush in my hand at the time – although I hadn't been aware of this before seeing the hand – and I used to turn the brush with the bristles below, and I'd bring it down with such a whack on this hand that it always disappeared. Then I'd wake up, and I'd feel all hot and flushed after it all.' I suggested she might have been hot and flushed in bed and that the dream was possibly intended to arouse her; she felt that might well be so.

One of my own recurring dreams used to be that of being trapped in a confined space, unable to get out, calling for help, but no one can hear me. Over the years a presentiment developed which warned me, should I be about to step into a lift, or go into a cellar: Look out or you'll be trapped! Anticipations of this kind tend to detract from the pull of the dream and once such a pattern of thought has begun the shock device is replaced by another. (This balancing operation of allowing the dreamer sufficient awareness to react to the happenings, but not enough to provoke reasoning about them, is one of the most subtle manipulations of dreaming.)

So far as possible, the forced awakening of the sleeper must be achieved by what would appear to be a logical development of the dream, the dreamer awakening in fear rather than bewilderment. I have often detected in my own dreams the preparation for a particular arousal shock suitable to certain malfunctions of old age, should such pose a danger to my sleeping self. I was having a pleasant dream of being in a spacious library, dipping into various books, when I turned to see a fireplace in the centre of the room, a nice coal-fire, and a big kettle boiling away on the top, an indication of tea about to be made. I imagine the Dream Mind simply took the handiest image it could – a kettle boiling on a fire – and set it in the middle of the library amongst books, knowing that few sights could have appealed more to me. At the same time, the cosy fire in a library, was the sign of a potentially dangerous situation – a conflagration. I was having a pleasant dream in which I was going round a vast art gallery with two famous painters, enjoying their comments on the paintings, when I spotted a few young shorthorn calves peep into the gallery. They looked timid enough, certainly no physical threat, but they did send a tremor through me, as I wondered what damage they might do in such a place.

In some dreams the preparatory period seems almost unrelated to the final arousal. I dream I am in the men's department of a rather grand shop, when I am asked by an assistant would I oblige a gentleman and his wife by trying on a coat – which they would like to see on someone else first. The dream went on for a long time, ending in my being unable to get my left arm into the sleeve of the coat – there was a protracted struggle, and I wake up, to find my left hand in a state of total numbness of cramp, a fairly common complaint during sleep, and so intense is it that I need to start rubbing the fingers and attempting to clutch and unclutch the hand to get the circulation going. In certain dreams the drama becomes centred upon one crucial issue as in the following dream.

I dream I meet a man who tells me that he is desperately in need of the sum of £2,400, and I agree to help him to get out of his trouble by buying certain securities from him. With these securities I now make a gamble, which wins me exactly £2,400; the profit from the deal, however, is not given me in money but is in a precious fluid contained in a small bowl. I decide to give the fluid and bowl to the man who was in difficulty, so that now he will be able to buy his securities back from me, and no one will be any worse off – seemingly a perfect solution. I put the bowl safely on a ledge, and ask a friend of the man where can I find him. He tells me where, and I explain to the friend that it is because I wish to give the bowl with the fluid worth £2,400, so that all his troubles will be over. The friend becomes eager and excited at the news, 'I will return it to him,' he says. 'No,' I say, 'bring him here and I'll give it to him into his hands.' But his friend is too eager, he doesn't heed me, picks up the bowl to hasten away with the good news, and as he takes hold of the bowl I get a foreboding of what may happen. He hurries to deliver his message of good tidings (the scene now becomes a dress circle in a theatre), and I see the bowl tilt, and as he makes to straighten it the whole thing falls from his hands – a complete loss. I waken up.

There are numerous forms of shock tactics employed in dreams to make the dreamer sit up and take notice, so to say, should the dream current happen to be running low at some moment of emergency, when it is essential to grab the dreamer's total attention. The following is an example: I had a dream in which I answer the telephone and hear a woman's voice, 'Hello, this is Marjorie!' (Marjorie being the wife of a dear friend). 'Oh hello, Marjorie! You sound in good form. And how is Alec?' 'He's dead,' she answers. 'Alec is dead.' I woke up at once with shock, and was upset for a time, until my own findings reassured me. That dream occurred a few years ago, and Alec is still alive and well, so is Marjorie, and had I not been aware of the shock tactic in dreams I should have been worried about my friends.

On occasion, when the need for arousal is urgent, an abrupt one is expedited. I was in a café waiting for my tea at what was to be the end of a long dream. A man opposite said, 'They are bringing your tea –' and he pulled a cord. Walls fell down all around me. I was alone and enclosed. For a moment I was full of alarm, then the thought struck me that it was the signal to wake me up for some reason. I began to yell and shout and woke up. I was overheated, with a pain in my side. I got out of bed and opened the window. I fell all right almost at once.

Although arousal is mostly achieved by a dream shock of some kind, it may be brought about by more gentle and subtle means, even by moral or social pressure, should the sleeper be responsive to such. I had a dream in which I had been visiting a quiet area of a museum, and feeling rather tired I had asked a man who was working there might I rest on a long bench. He said I could, but not for long. I laid myself down on my back on the bench, and the rest to my limbs was one of exquisite pleasure. But after a short time I felt the man tapping me on the shoulder, indicating it was closing time, and that I had better get up. Oh what a struggle it is going to be, I thought, to lift myself out of sleep, and to get up – but I suppose there is nothing else for it, and with painful discipline I forced myself to waken up and slowly rise from the seat. As I did so I became aware of waking up, and found myself lying on my back in my own bed. I was very warm, my head buried in the pillow, and light fresh morning air coming in through the open window. I felt well and, unusual for me, rather comfortably sleepy. Yet I realised I had sunk low down in the bed, and I found it difficult to rise up. Then I recalled the dream, and spotted the almost identical feelings, one of rising from a flat bench, the other of being sunk down in bed. The only danger may have been that I was in a most vulnerable position, one from which it would have been difficult to rouse myself and get up in case of a sudden danger (that, most likely, is why our dreaming is more vivid when lying supine instead of on one side or the other). I had a dream in which I am one of a small party of four, being driven in a horse carriage through the 'streets' of Venice, and then to finish off we go into the sea, the horse taking us on a circular tour of the bay. I see little of all this, and I am lying down on the floor of the carriage, my head partly covered. I wake up and find I am lying flat on my stomach and the bedclothes are over my head. I believed every single moment of that dream for it all felt so true.

The most vivid example of the warning mechanism in dreaming, although not seen as such, is the nightmare. It should be understood that the more terrifying the nightmare, the more devils, demons and ogres there are around, and the more grisly and revolting the details and happenings, the more concerned your Dream Mind has been about you. Nightmares occur at some time or other to every dreamer, but most frequently to those who take alcohol, sedatives or drugs; the reason for this is that when sleep has been overladen with hypnotics, the normal dreaming function of arousal fails to work, so that dreams of a more violent character are needed to awaken the sleeper. Coleridge tells of a nightmare in which a woman was attempting to pluck out his right eye; he then goes on to say that when he awoke his right eyelid actually swelled up. We can be fairly sure that his eyelid was swollen during sleep, and that the nightmare was a response to it – a swollen eyelid is difficult to ignore during wakefulness – yet even a mind so intelligent as his could make a mistaken assumption about a dream. Such dreams are of course most frightening, but although the nightmare may aggravate palpitations, sweating, and a sense of having one's ribs crushed, it does not initiate the basic dysfunction but simply dramatises it.

Once the dreamer grasps the nature of the arousal function in dreaming, the horror of a near nightmare, whilst it serves swiftly to arouse, may even assume a comic nature when thought over later, as it did in the following dream. I dream I am driving late on a Saturday night along a side street in the West End, and feeling uneasy in what I take to be a sordid area at this hour I want to get away. I stop at traffic lights, they turn green, but when I press the accelerator the car reverses, and the street is suddenly full of children, and I am afraid I might hit one. I manage to turn the car up a narrow street, drive into another street, and go down a short steep hill. Thank goodness I'm away, I think, but the next thing I see is that it is a cul-de-sac and I can go no further. I now attempt to turn the car but fail, and I get out, and start talking to a printer on night work when he calls, 'Look out!' There is a lot of fluttering from a huge sack near the wall – apparently there is a dangerous eagle inside it. People dash off screaming as I and the printer dodge to safety in a doorway behind a thick curtain. The strange bird or other creature can be heard scuttering around outside, and I pray that it won't find us. The next moment the curtain parts and the 'eagle' looks in. It is like a huge, black and hairy gorilla, with wings, a bird's beak, but the face of a man. I woke up with the shock of fear. But when I recalled that ridiculous bogey figure the Dream Mind had botched together to scare me, despite a certain thrill in feeling so frightened, I could not help but burst out laughing. The softer the mattress and the heavier the bedclothes the more difficult for the dream shock to arouse the sleeper, because the essential reaction of producing vocal sounds sufficient to pierce the torpor and alert the senses is more difficult, with the dreamer in a state of sleep paralysis.

# 6

## *Wish Fulfilment or Fobbing Off?*

I have had numerous dreams that began as wish fulfilment but the fulfilment was repeatedly promised and never fulfilled, and they all ended up with a fobbing off. The reason for this, I shall explain at once, is that sexual desire cannot be fully realised in a dream without arousing the dreamer, thirst cannot be quenched by dream water nor hunger satisfied by dream food – 'It shall even be as when a hungry man dreameth, and behold, he eateth; but he awaketh, and his soul is empty: or as when a thirsty man dreameth, and behold, he is faint, and his soul hath appetite.'

My own indisposition was that of becoming overheated in bed. Over a long period I suffered from disc trouble, and as warmth eased it, I would heat the electric blanket under the sheet until the bed was very warm. I also had a complaint which occasioned feverish bouts, and the combination, aggravated by my habit of writing down dreams, resulted in my getting hot in the head, as well as in the body. The following are examples from a series of dreams that responded to my thermal stimulus.

*Dream*: I am back in London, living in our St George's Square flat, and feeling hot and sweaty, I decide to go into the nearby block of flats, Dolphin Square, to have a swim. I go straight to the usual pool on the lowest floor but find it has gone, and a porter tells me that it has been moved to the top floor. I go up in the lift to the top floor, and look around but cannot find the pool, and am told by another porter that it is now on the third floor. I go along there, see the swim pool, but it is empty, not a drop of water in it. I am getting hotter, and I ask a porter if any of the showers are working; he tells me they are, and directs me to them. Wearing trunks I go to cool down under a shower, see the taps marked *A* and *B*, and after I turn each tap out comes a gush of hot water. A woman, large and matronly, has been watching, and seems to be gazing admiringly at my chest; I explain to her my predicament – no cold water, and I need a cooling shower. She suggests that I go with her to her flat and enjoy one there. I seldom refuse an invitation, and go off with her, eyeing her perhaps more warily than speculatively, for although she is not sexually unattractive, what I am looking for is a good cool shower. She takes me to her flat, leads me to the magnificent bathroom, turns on the shower tap, sets it on cold and suggests I try it. I eagerly go under, and the water pours down on me. Odd, I think, as I stand there, this is a cold shower, but for some reason it's not cooling me. Then I spot what I take to be the cause – I have left my shirt on, which I gather is waterproof, and so I have to get out from under and take it off. Stripped of my shirt, I return to my shower, but the water suddenly stops. 'Yes,' explains the matron, 'it's just eleven o'clock, and all the water is always cut off at eleven prompt.' I wake up hot and sweating. The following is another example of the same 'fobbing off' tactic.

*Dream*: I am back in the Bolton of my childhood on a sultry day, feeling hot and longing to cool down. I go off to a familiar stretch of water near the moorland, where once I went often to swim, and start stripping off, anticipating as I do the pleasure it will be. However, I am just about to go in when a gamekeeper turns up and informs me the water has been contaminated, and no bathers are allowed in. Disappointed but persistent, I now set off for an open-air swim pool I knew as a boy, but at the entrance there is a notice stating that the pool has been closed down. Hotter than ever, and longing even more for a swim, I make off for the sea. I imagine I can actually smell the brine, but when I get to the beach I find only muddy sand, the tide being out. The dream continues – and I go off once more, and finally reach a large pool in the country. The sight delights me, and I hurry to get my clothes off and my swim trunks on. There are a few youths and a woman in the pool, and now, ready for my dip, I pause at the edge of the clear cool water before diving, raise my hands, and am about to plunge in when I spot a grey form down in the water. Panic fills me, and I manage to draw back, as I see this grey form joined by others. Now I can make out dozens of octopuses. How lucky I am to escape! I feel I must warn the others, and I look towards the woman swimmer, who is unaware of the danger, but am too frightened to go in and save her, and I feel ashamed of my fear. I am about to call out when I see the young bathers diving in to go to her help.

The white bodies of the swimmers can be seen in the water, in amongst the darker grey shapes of the octopuses. My thirst is forgotten. The next moment I wake up. I am hot, sweating and weary.

I believe that in both instances I was asleep in bed and overheated, and the varying dream situations promised alleviation. My dream self was engaged by hope, followed by disappointment, a further promise, again disappointment – a pattern familiar to me in life. The prospect was enhanced by the anticipation of plunging my overheated body into cold water. Why should these various setbacks occur in a dream? Because the Dream Mind, in its artifice of creating an imaginary duplication of conscious life, must pursue a course in which the poise is held between the train of dream imagery created to absorb the stimuli inimical to sleep, and the dreamer's reaction and degree of credulity to the same. To preserve sleep in my own case, there was a necessity to divert attention from being overheated, yet without the dream becoming a nightmare. The more sleep was prolonged the more overheating became insupportable and threatened to interrupt it. The dream action was intensified to occupy and divert; but this animation made me even hotter, and so anticipation had to be raised again and again: *Try another floor for the pool!* or *Just ahead is a pool of cool water in which you can bathe!*

Dreamers are often impressed by the fantastic sights and happenings in dreams, but what needs to be pointed out is that almost any imaginary sensation or happening can occur in a dream. The dreamer can float up into heaven or down into hell, he can become the devil with horns, or an angel with wings, he can witness the universe being blown up by a nuclear bomb, with everyone lying dead and rising to life again. There is no limit to what can be displayed in a dream, but as has been explained, no matter what the various stratagems may be, one thing the dream cannot do is feed and satisfy a hungry person, or quench the thirst of a thirsty one, or cool an overheated one.

Why can the Dream Mind raise the dead, persuade the dreamer he is actually flying over high buildings, yet fail to convince the dreamer that he is diving into a pool of cold water? Because raising a person from the dead in dreams asks for nothing more than a visual image, the manipulation of the faculty of sight, which is implicit in dreaming itself; the same being true of flying – the sensation will be assumed by the dreamer. Miracles of every kind are available in dreams – any phenomenon which imagination alone can produce the dream will supply, but to physical needs it can only sham a response. Every apparent development in a dream is no more than an instant stratagem to circumvent some imminent threat to sleep – or, if need be, to shock the sleeper awake.

Why octopuses? Octopuses with their eight arms set around the mouth, each arm with its fleshy suckers, and the large frightening eyes, make a gripping dream image, one to inspire terror. But why should octopuses appear near the end of the dream? Because the pressures of heat and thirst were increasing, and at the last moment the Dream Mind, by use of octopuses, produced a sudden shock – another instinctive distraction – which for a time overrode the nagging demands of heat. Fear was succeeded by a sense of relief at having been spared the ordeal of the octopuses. All this occupied the imagination and kept my mind off the discomfort. Suppose the Dream Mind had allowed me to dive into the water? Since it was beyond its power to have produced the consequent cooling of my body, there would have been an immediate mental reaction: *Why am I not cool?* In which case an instantly plausible excuse would be intimated, such as the water being warm because the pond was attached to an electricity cooling station. By this time, however, in both dreams, my body was becoming hotter, and may have insisted on being cooled, and this forced itself on the senses, precipitating arousal.

I am convinced that fear fulfilment is a more common and impelling motive power in dreaming than is wish fulfilment – the anxious mother worried over the safety of her child, the wife apprehensive of her husband's safety on some dangerous work, the family learning that Mother has to have an operation – each one of these will ensure ready pockets of emotions to be tapped for dreams. I had a friend who often told me of his extreme reluctance to spend money: 'I dislike very much the idea of signing a cheque, and put it off as long as I can,' he would say, 'but as for paying in actual money, I find it too painful; I know it amounts to the same in the long run, but even the smallest amount I pay by cheque.' My friend told his dreams to me, and the following is a recurring dream that plagued him, and even though he could sense it coming on he said that he always fell for it.

He is in Harrods of Knightsbridge, looking around and enjoying watching others spending money, while he keeps a grip on his own. The next thing he meets up with an aristocratic dame, a lavish spender, and finds himself going from one department to another, in awe at the grand manner with which she spends money, buying anything that catches her eye, jewellery and furs and the like, with complete disregard for the expense, and at the same time handing him the parcels to carry. Although impressed by her prodigality, he wonders why he is even bothering to stay with her and carry all the purchases around, as her manner towards him is so overbearing. The dream goes on for a long time, my friend laden down with her purchases, until finally she has all the parcels taken from him and carried out to a waiting taxi. She doesn't say a word of thanks, and with a sense of relief he sees her drive off. Then before he quite realises what is happening, he finds himself ushered to the cash desk by a salesman, the bill thrust in his hand for the total, for which he has to get out his chequebook and pay. The worst of it all, he told me, was that the grand lady was never much to look at in the first place.

On the other hand, the following is a verbatim account of what I heard from a woman who works evenings in an hotel: 'This Madge that I work with behind the bar,' she told me, 'is a widow, with no family, an' though she's gettin' on a bit, it seems she's still attractive to men like, the way they look at her an' talk to her. Now I was chattin' to her one night after closin' time, we're washin' glasses, see, an' we got on to the subject like, an' Madge, who lives alone says to me: "Well I've slept wi' every kind of man under the sun – young blacks, Swedes, Italians, Frenchies, a Chinese or two – you name 'um an' I've 'ad 'um, the lot. I fancy a different one every night I do." Eh, it quite alarmed me, the way she came out with it. "But Madge," I says to her, "is it not a bit dangerous like, I mean to say, you livin' on your own now, meeting strange men, an' then there's the neighbours to think about?" "Eh, there's no danger," she says, "I only 'ave 'um in my dreams. I've not had one in the flesh for years. But I no sooner get my head on yon' pillow an' go off to sleep an' a chap comes up. I'll bet I 'ave one tonight, but what he'll be I can't say until he turns up. You see, in dreams you've got to take what's sent.'"

7

## Recall – Research – Retribution

### Dream Recall

How much you recall of your dreaming, in what detail and with what clarity, depends upon your aptitude, your familiarity with imaginational experience, and the interest you take in your dream life. Should you be introspective, responsive to your own daydreams and ideas, often to the exclusion of all else – as should happen with writers and artists generally – means that you can keep your attention focused on some wisp of thought that has crossed your mind, and turn from any task to give it your attention. Dream recall will also depend on what kind of sleeper you are and how often you wake up during the night, and what your mental orientation is when you wake up – it needs to be inward, to what you have dreamt, not what tasks await you. If you share a bed, and a few words are exchanged on awakening, your dreams will evanesce, and the most interesting details will be lost. Going off somewhere to write down dreams is possible, but a dream is best caught *in situ*; the further you get from the bed the swifter the dream fades away. I became good at dream recall from years of keeping a detailed journal, when I learnt to capture the elusive image or idea, and wrote down scores of dreams. (Muslims, a thousand years ago, rated dreams as worthy of one quarter of an autobiography, which struck me as about right.)

Should you have an inclination to study your dream life, I would recommend that you compose yourself some time before going to bed, take off day clothes, exercise a little, possibly take a bath, avoid distractions and try to keep an empty mind. Make sure there is a large open writing pad and pens handy beside the bed, and on lying down to sleep shed so far as possible all external worries, and take up a sensitive awareness of what you hope to engage in – *sleep*. You will lie there in the dark, anticipating the engagement about to take place between your imagination and the Dream Mind, rather like an audience in a theatre on which a hush falls when it prepares to give itself up to play or film – what Jung calls the *rite d'entrée*, when preparing for some special experience. In this way you soon become conditioned and switched on for dreaming. On awakening, do not concentrate hard, but try to light upon one single episode of the dream – a hint will often lead you to the whole dream. But *never* should a dream be taken as other than what it is – a purely imaginary string of happenings devised solely to monitor sleep. (By what other means could Nature contrive to keep in contact with the sleeper?) At certain periods I have gone to bed and deliberately switched off, as the combination of dreaming and study of dreams can be tiring, an activity for which the mind is not geared. At such times I always sleep much better, am often unable to remember any of my early dreams, but during the second sleep, usually from five o'clock onwards, can always recall dreams but let them fade away

## Research

'You're writing a book on dreaming?' a doctor friend remarked to me, and I agreed I was. 'But where can you do your research,' he went on, ' – here in the Isle of Man?' 'In bed,' I told him. From the look he gave me I gathered that he was not impressed. Oddly enough, not only was it perfectly true, but I would suggest that anyone interested in pursuing dream research will find the best laboratory is his own bedroom, and night the most fertile period for dream insights. There is a reassuring comment in the Hobson book: 'The importance of Hervey de Saint-Denis lies in his emphasis on the self as a scientific instrument.' The laboratory may smack of science, but dreaming does not lend itself to detached scrutiny. The fact is, once you take a bath you may feel fresher, but you forfeit dream percipience. I would recommend that anyone taking up a writer's life – plays, poems, stories or novels – ought not get out of a dressing gown until noon at the earliest. (I'm afraid that from habit I mostly do so, but my best days are those in which I go straight from my bed to the nearby room where I do most of my writing)

Rumination, of course, is best pursued lying down; often during the night, when I have been up, and am writing a dream as I stand beside a high chest of drawers on which I keep blotter and notebooks, the mental energy may start to wane, in which case I go back to bed and write *lying down* – not sitting up. Anyone prepared to lie awake for an hour or two in the dark at night, relaxed and unfussed, with a notebook and pencil and light at hand, will solve many of his or her problems (but may not sleep as soundly). For any novelist suffering from what is called 'writer's block' – personally, I regard this less as an affliction than a hint to the writer that he or she has taken up misconceived writing intentions – I would recommend a spell of sleeping alone, with a substantial hardback foolscap book on hand. Then on waking up during the night getting out of bed at once, sitting at the table on which the manuscript has been carefully arranged the previous evening, and starting writing at once. The sleepier one feels, the more uninclined for the task, the better the writing will flow once there has been some mental stirring; this is a diverting of the imaginative energy from dreaming to another form of fiction.

## Retribution

This familiarity with my dream life, and the fact that I had often picked up play pointers from dreams, may have given me the rash notion that instead of mere poaching from dreams I might go on to manipulating the dream intelligence – this in the days long before I knew about the Dream Mind. I had agreed to write the film scripts of two of my own plays, and I found that on certain mornings the imaginative current would dry up at some difficult scene. It was my habit after a light lunch to doze off for an hour, and now I decided I would turn my mind on to the scene, to see if the dream would produce an answer. I was often successful, but on waking up an hour later it seemed that the best bits of dialogue were forgotten. I became more determined, and one day had pencil and paper on hand so as to get the details down as they came. I was lying there, on the threshold of sleep, precariously balancing the traces of consciousness against the slowly enveloping somnolent cloud, insinuating the scene into the picture and pretending I was falling naturally to sleep, but keeping a furtive ray of thought on the dream. As my conscious awareness dimmed, and the imagination was taken over, I kept the script scene in mind, so that it might merge with what the reverie brought. As soon as I had got as much of the new development as I judged I could hold, and felt close to being drawn against my will into sleep, I summoned all my determination and managed to escape, sat up and swiftly wrote it down, keeping mainly to dialogue, which is what counts. I felt pleased with myself, not only at having got it down, but in overcoming the powerful desire for sleep. I'll use that again I thought – match my wits against Morpheus. The dodge worked for me again, and gave me a lead of which I had never thought before. Once again it demanded extreme willpower during that hypnagogic period, to play the mind against the instinct of sleep, but I managed it. The next time – these were not successive days – I got the best ideas I had ever had for a play. Once I got over the difficult part of sitting up to write, which on this occasion proved easier than expected, I found myself writing scene after scene, the whole thing flowing effortlessly, the dialogue natural, and no sign of a headache. This is really marvellous, I thought to myself as I wrote away – I have at last mastered it.

Then I felt myself being shaken, looked up and saw it was my wife, 'You told me to waken you,' she said. 'But I've been awake some time,' I said, 'I've been writing away.' I looked at the pad and pencil and to my astonishment and dismay saw they hadn't been touched. It got one across me then, I said to myself, but I'll watch it next time. But there was to be no next time, for next day the moment I laid myself down to rest I became disoriented – out of touch with whether I was awake or asleep. The same chaotic feelings sprang up day after day, as though I had a series of dreams within dreams, nightmares and hallucinations, until my mental state became such that I was no longer sure when I was actually awake whether I was awake or not. I found myself wandering about in a confused state of near daydreaming, bemoaning my loss of clarity of mind, and I began to dread what up until then had been a joy – my brief afternoon sleep. I gave up at once any further considerations of that trick. Then as I slowly recovered my lucidity, it seemed as I was about to take my rest, I got an awareness of a large Presence, looming up beside me whispering, 'You aren't thinking of playing any more games on me, are you?' It may only have been imagination, but if it was Morpheus, I realised that the god of dreams was not to be trifled with, and I promised I wasn't and wouldn't.

# 8

## *Dream Impulsion*

The most ingenious accomplishment of the Dream Mind is the taking up of some morsel of feeling, together with a few recent impressions, and shaping the whole into a dream – often of a novel kind and with a surprise ending that awakens the dreamer. The following dream is one I had a long time after I had worked on a television serial, the standard of which seemed deplorable to me, but as we were badly in need of money I did my best and kept the sense of shame to myself. This experience gave me a soured feeling about writing for television, aggravated by a few further serial scripts I wrote that were set around a newspaper office.

*Dream*: I find that against my better judgement I have signed an agreement to plan the format and write the first scripts of a television series that is to be set around a newspaper office. A big publicity party has been arranged to celebrate the inauguration ceremony, and I am there with mixed feelings which I must keep strictly to myself. At first there had been the anticipation of earning money for easy work – but now this feeling has worn off, yet having taken the job there is nothing for me but to get on with it, and join in all the celebrations with an air of bogus heartiness. At the height of the party, our hostess, the woman who is running the publicity for the television company, insists that we all go quiet and listen to the latest smash hit record from America – one not out here yet, one you can't get hold of, but a terrific hit in New York, known as 'The Sick Record'. So we all crowd around, everybody merry, laughing, talking and drinking, to hear the record as the woman puts it on. The record begins to play, but instead of music and singing it turns out to be a record of the best American artistes, singers, actors and others, all famous, being sick and vomiting. And as the people at the party listen, they all go quiet for a time, and the next thing, everybody – but particularly myself – starts making sounds of being sick and begins to vomit all over the place.

Insomnia is not only an aid in recalling dreams, but is also a good state for hatching a few. On one occasion I had a pain in my shoulder, and to ease it I put on a wool shirt in place of a pyjama jacket, which caused me to feel overheated. I woke up after sleeping about two hours, and then, instead of getting up as I usually do, I decided to keep warm in bed, and lay awake for three hours. Before going to bed I had switched on the radio and heard of the American landing in Grenada, and discussions as to why Britain, the Queen and the Prime Minister, had not first been informed of the intention. When I fell asleep I dreamt of being with a number of friends in a room, when I got this peculiar weightless feeling, and I began to demonstrate to them how I could levitate and glide around

– and lying flat, gazing up at the ceiling, I began to float around the room. I couldn't see their faces, but assumed they were all watching and suitably impressed, and I thought to myself, 'You'll be all right so long as you avoid hitting any objects.' I woke up briefly, the floating dream vividly in my mind – I did not write it down – then I had the following dream.

*Dream*: There has been an early evening drinks party at our home, and now I have just seen the last of our friends off, and feeling rather hungry, and looking forward to our meal, I go back in the front door of what appears to be our present home, but it is much larger and situated in London. As I walk into the house I notice strangers walking in casually beside me, and to my apprehension find it is becoming crowded with people I don't know. They are moving around in a boisterous fashion, dozens of them, with vivid faces, lively expressions and loud voices. As I maunder around perplexed, I am aware of every scrap of conversation, yet no one is taking any notice of me, as though I were someone in the lobby of a busy hotel. Although I feel the obligation not to offend a visitor under my roof, it seems odd and rather trying to feel such a stranger in my own home. Slowly I gather that they are a coach party of American tourists who, by mistake it seems, have taken our house to be their accommodation at Dolphin Square nearby. I go from room to room, looking for my wife to help me bring some order, and get things right, but I can't find her. She's always missing, I think, when she's most wanted. I start attempting vainly to explain the situation to various groups, but there is so much bustle and loud talk that I am interrupted and nobody gives me much attention. It's strange, I keep thinking, how you can be made feel out of place in your own home – at the same time I feel it would be unforgivable to offend anyone. I go into the kitchen and come across a group of youngsters, seated round a table eating our chicken stew, and I try to explain to them, feeling ashamed of myself as I do so: 'Don't you see,' I tell them, 'you are in the wrong place – and you are eating our evening meal.' The youngsters, surprisingly and with more understanding than others, show sympathy, but it seems there is nothing they can do about it, and they go on eating.

In the lounge there are many new arrivals, and I go up to one, a big American with an old wrinkled face, a man of some authority, and I start explaining to him in a quiet manner that they have made a mistake, that this is no hotel but our home. He turns on me in a temper, takes hold of me by the hair and glaring at me yells out: 'I don't wanna hear again that we're in the wrong place! Got me?' And giving me a final shake he puts me aside. I feel helpless and very sorry for myself, and go about uncertain what to do. At last I find some people who are sympathetic and understanding, and prepared to listen, although no one seems eager to leave: 'Everybody listen – please listen –' I call out. 'Listen to the gentleman,' says a woman. 'I'm sorry,' I tell them, 'I hate to say this to you – but you have been brought to the wrong place –' I awake at this moment, find that I am extremely hot both in head and body, and I get up and cool down under a tepid shower.

The Dream Mind is remarkable at exploiting any feelings

which have had to be repressed. The following dream occurred after Christmas, when I had the onerous duty of writing letters of thanks for various Christmas presents I had received, most of which were of no use to me. I cannot bring myself to disconcert those who have taken pains to please me, yet I will not write anything actually untrue or wholly insincere, so that each letter demanded discretion to express thanks under such restrictions: 'It was awfully good of you – what splendid nuts!' I found myself writing, and: 'The wine looks very good indeed,' and: 'The chocolates will be enjoyed – ' I did not add, but not by myself.

*Dream*: I am getting out of a coach in the Charing Cross Road outside the Garrick Theatre, one of a mixed party. I don't feel too happy about being one of a mixed party, since neither the men nor the woman feel free to speak their minds, but about this I can do nothing. The arrangement is that we first have dinner at the theatre and then go to the play, but the woman courier tells us that there is a half an hour to spare, and suggests we go across the road to the pub for a drink. I rather dislike what seems to be the artificial atmosphere of most London pubs, but go to the pub, where a hearty chap in the party takes me in tow, and tells me he's going to look after me. In the pub I meet a friend who asks me if it will be all right if he comes with us to the theatre, even though he has not been invited. I tell him that it will, but it gives me an uneasy feeling. Meanwhile my hearty friend has ordered beer and salads, and he is eating a huge plate of green salad and cold beef as the barman starts filling my plate. I say, 'But we're going to eat shortly!' 'Get it down you,' my friend says, 'a salad will do you no harm.' The barman starts piling my plate with lettuce, which I feel will cause me flatulence. 'Not too much,' I tell him. 'Shut up,' says my hearty pal, 'I'll have to pay the same price no matter how much he puts on. Now what about these trousers I've got us?' He has one leg into a pair of grey flannel trousers, and offers me the other side of the open trouser top. I feel it would be churlish to refuse him, although I am satisfied with my own trousers. I take my trousers off and put my right leg into one trouser leg, with his leg in the other. 'How's that for a fit?' he says. 'It's all right,' I say, yet I feel there is something not right about the arrangement. 'But how are we going to walk,' I ask, 'like in a three-legged race?' 'What's wrong with that?' he says. I pull my leg out, feeling ungrateful but relieved, and put my trousers back on. I look at my watch and see that it is just after seven o'clock, time to go, and yet I haven't touched the salad or the beer.

The next thing we are crowding down into a combined kitchen-restaurant in the basement of the theatre, about to have our meal before going to see the play. I do not like the prospect of eating a meal before seeing a play, nor am I favourably impressed by the easygoing atmosphere, as I see a big woman lifting up huge steaks, red and raw, and using a pair of scissors to trim off portions to suit each patron. 'Not too large for me,' I tell her, as she displays an enormous piece of steak. 'How's that?' she asks, cutting off a piece. 'Still a bit too large,' I say. She starts trimming it down without further asking, but cutting off what look to me like all the best portions. Finally she is left with a small piece which is all gristle and fat. 'Just a minute,' I tell her, 'I can't eat that.' A plump, untidy young woman, a friend of the woman cutting the steak, has come up as we are standing there; she goes to a shelf and takes a chamber pot down, lifts up her dress, pulls down her knickers, and sits on the pot and starts a fairly loud bowel action. I like a bit of informality, I think, but this seems a bit too much. I feel I ought to turn away like a gentleman, but somehow I find I don't turn away and also feel rather ashamed of myself. When she has done she stands up, adjusts her underclothes, shakes herself down, gets a sheet of paper to cover the pot, and remarks, 'I suppose by rights I didn't ought to have done it here in the kitchen.' The steak woman now turns to me but I chance to awake at that moment – rather to my relief.

# 9

# *Symbols and Sovereigns*

The symbol, an ancient representation or token, has a suggestive rather than a direct connotation, it evokes emotion rather than reason, which makes it an ideal medium for use in dreams. A symbol may hint at much that eludes the word in the same way that a look can often imply more than the tongue can express, the unspoken message leaving a more lasting impression. 'The best possible expressions of something as yet unknown,' Jung wrote of symbols, '– bridges thrown out towards an invisible shore.' Which suits the protracted course of the dream, with its often indeterminate ending. Realisation in dreams, as in religion, is never truly fulfilled, or intended to be, since apprehension and celestial anticipation serve better. There is no problem affecting a dreamer to which the Dream Mind will not respond, from solving the quests of scientists, supplying ideas for poems, plays and novels, even to that of Marcus Aurelius, who was able to find in dreams what he sought. 'That by the agency of dreams,' he writes, 'I was given antidotes both of other kinds and against the spitting of blood and vertigo.'

Therefore, the Dream Mind, aware of our every thought and fancy, and particularly those ideas associated with dreaming and dream interpretation, will plant numerous 'symbols' in a dream, simply to grip the sleeper all the more by creating an extra strand of involvement. If the dreamer believes that asparagus, balloons, boxes, clarinets and so on, have a sexual symbolism, then of course their presence in a dream will appear significant. The dream switches from one area to a wholly unrelated one, yet instils the shift with a mimetic correspondence which may seem ridiculous but works.

I dreamt of a friend who talks much of writers and writing, who was leading me along a maze of streets behind Fleet Street on our way to see an editor. 'It's just a paragraph along here,' he said, 'turn left, a couple of short sentences and we are there.' Then he explained, 'I no longer use the old measures of distances, such as yards or miles, but see distances in sentences or paragraphs or even chapters.' It seemed a plausible idea to me during the dream. Much that is taken to be sexual symbolism is simply a form of dream parody. I have had dreams in which I was attempting to get water out of my ears after a swim, to waken up and find I had a need to pass water. I will not pursue these Freudian or other conjectures, except to say that anyone with unsatisfied sexual desires will not fail to find 'symbols' to match, from putting the key into the lock as he enters his home, grasping a doorknob, taking hat off and exposing head, standing umbrella on stand, taking raincoat off and putting finger through the loop as he hangs it up, and so on. Any instinctive desire proliferates in allusions.

Symbols in dreams, I would suggest, very often do not

present some unconscious or repressed sexual urge in a more acceptable guise, but appear in dreams mainly because of their innate and mysterious significance in human consciousness from earliest time. The so-called sexual symbol, such as that of a snake rearing up and hissing as it is about to strike, has a more dramatic effect upon the dreamer than would the sexual part or act it is said to represent. Phallic worship by the Greeks and others was hardly a disguise of the generative organ, so much as a glorification, in the form of a fertility rite. We need to keep in mind what the dream function is – a fantasy, mainly of visual expedients, to beguile the imagination during sleep so as to produce reactions in the dreamer. The operation demands a train of extempore images to sustain the immediacy of the dream happenings, and this is best served by visual means. The sexual act, occurring mostly at night, usually in the dark, is alive with tactile sensations, but these are not easily simulated in dreaming, nor is the sense of smell. The genitalia, male or female, have but scant visual allure, and copulation none that would animate a dream.

In sexual dreams, as in cabaret or the like, the suggestive or evocative – or indeed the symbol, from an old boot to a bicycle – may serve the purpose, essentially preludial, of exciting erotic interest, more keenly than could the actual thing or act it is said to symbolise. Repression is a significant inciter of dreaming, of course, but it need not be sexual. Behaviour often taken to be the outcome of repression may itself be a counter fulfilment of desire. Any unuttered wish, thought or feeling, tends to turn up in dreams – an emotional skeleton in the cupboard – and as feelings and stray thoughts associated with sex appear to be those most frequently demanding to be kept to oneself, they come up most often in dreams. Their sexuality is incidental to their quality of intimacy and privacy; these are the real dream determinants. Few artists have felt the need to portray carnal intercourse – no matter how indifferent they were to the reaction of others – since eroticism can better be suggested by the symbol or external sign. The symbol, I feel sure, a vital element of man's preliterate culture, is alive in our dreams because it is of the Archemind, the source of all creative expression, and one with the spawn from which our dreams are hatched.

Sovereigns, and most royal personages in dreams are analogous to symbols, in that a crown, a uniform, and decorations connote a certain authority. What makes them particularly apt for dream characters is that their faces, being so familiar from newspapers and television, their images are easily evoked, and the appearance of a royal person in a dream will at once pep up any flagging interest. I had a dream that I was on the Underground, travelling from Victoria to Sloane Square, and found myself seated next to Prince Philip. First I had to peek sideways just to make sure I wasn't mistaken, but the nose and the general bearing made it obvious. His very presence there beside me, of which I could not be other than highly aware, created such a significant interest that it carried the dream along for a time without need of action. I kept wondering what he was doing on an underground train, and felt myself indulging a certain conceit that he should be seated next to me. I'm not the sort of chap to be impressed by royalty, I kept telling myself, yet no doubt others will be when I tell them. The drama really picked up when suddenly he turned and spoke to me, and asked if I would like a pair of tickets for the Cup Final at Wembley. Of course they can get tickets when we can't, I thought, and probably the poor chap doesn't want to go. Nor did I, for that matter, but since it was Prince Philip who had asked me, and as the tickets were said to be in enormous demand, I said I'd be very glad of them. I was aware of being rather short of money at the time, and against my better judgement I asked him how much they would be. He turned on me, pained that I should have even brought up such a sordid subject: 'Oh we aren't allowed to touch money!' he exclaimed. He said it in a way that implied any well-bred person ought to have known such a fact. Not allowed to touch money, I thought, what an interesting custom, it seemed to add a touch of St Francis to royalty. I never got the tickets – he dropped the subject after my gaffe, and I considered myself to have been mildly snubbed, which I felt served me jolly well right for being so brash. But at least he did nod to me as he got out in Sloane Square. He has only a short walk to Buckingham Palace, I thought, so it's a handy stop, but what a pity I opened my big mouth about money!

Such a short journey on the underground train, little happened, yet what did happen, because it was Prince Philip, I found heady, and even when I awoke I felt quite bucked up about such a familiar contact with a member of the royal family, it being a refreshing change from the usual proletarian characters that people most of my dreams. I happened to be feeling especially fit at the time, and wondered had the sanguine state of health and spirits something to do with that dream treat. The following is another dream of the same class.

*Dream*: I find myself inside Buckingham Palace, where I have been invited to dine with the Queen. It is in a small side room, a sort of kitchen, and the Queen is saying to me, 'I thought I'd invite you, Bill, so that the talk would be easy, our having met before. There'll only be four of us.' (I had once met the Queen's sister, Princess Margaret, at a premiere of a play of mine, and she and I and my wife chatted away for some twenty minutes during the interval.) Actually, there were five at table, two mates of mine, and the Queen and Prince Philip. He was on my left, and during the dream he changed into Prince Charles, who was especially nice and chatty. Steak, large portions but cut thin, was spread out ready for cooking. I was quite happy to be there, but I had had my tea, and didn't feel hungry – in fact fell full, and wondered how I would get my steak down. I suppose I'll have to do the same as I've always done on these occasions, I thought, just chew and swallow it and hope it rests nicely on my stomach. Posh folk would invite you when you've already had your tea – that always happens. I kept up a lively chat with the Queen and the atmosphere was relaxed. A noise woke me up. I found that my stomach felt swollen and most uncomfortable – from having eaten sprouts, which never agree with me. I would conjecture that the feeling of indigestion tended to inhibit sleep, and to overcome this royalty had to be brought on.

# 10

# *Hypnosis and Dreaming*

'The psycho-physiological conditions of sleep, dreams and hypnosis are in all probability essentially alike –' Hobson in *The Dreaming Brain* quotes this comment of Wilhelm Wundt. Such was my own startling impression, simply from observing the phenomenon of hypnosis a number of times from the front row in a theatre. A crucial period for Freud was that spent in Paris, at the age of thirty, when he studied for some months under the famous neurologist Charcot, and became acquainted with that man's extraordinary cures by use of hypnosis. Although Freud retained a deep respect for Charcot, and an interest in hypnotism – 'the royal road to the unconscious' – in *The Interpretation of Dreams* he carefully avoids the subject, making only four scant references. Having introduced his own psychoanalytical methods, and given 'the royal road' to dreaming, he clearly intended to dissociate the two. Freud said that his own dream theory had killed the psychology taught by Wundt, although Wundt did not think so: 'In reality all which in these phenomena [sleep and dreams] suggest an esoteric explanation can without difficulty be explained psychologically and physiologically; but those things which cannot be explained this way will always be demonstrated to be, on closer examination, either superstition or auto-illusions.'

Hypnotism is certainly a remarkable performance to watch – to see how in moments a group of people can set aside all commonsense, and become the dupes of an ordinary little man, prompting them to engage in the most absurd roles. I had no idea how like dreaming it was until I watched a score of men and women volunteers, mostly between the ages of eighteen and thirty, who went on the stage perfectly normal – one was a man from the next seat to mine, with whom I had been chatting – and within minutes were all acting like puppets. They were seated downstage in a row, facing the audience, and reacting to every suggestion the hypnotist made, the following being among a wide variety of situations they were involved in, and to which they gave vivid response.

The hypnotist told them that each one had won £100,000, at which they gave whoops of joy; then he suggested that they should all go to the races and put the money on a horse that the hypnotist knew must win. This they believe they do, and they imagine they are at the racecourse, and yell with excitement throughout the imaginary race, as the hypnotist hives a running commentary. They dance around with delight when on the final stretch the hypnotist tells them their horse leads the field. Then he calls out that another horse is coming up, and they start crying out in a frenzy to their own horse. It is a photo finish, and some of them literally bite their nails waiting for the verdict. Then they learn that their own horse has lost the race, they moan and sigh and shed tears onstage; next he tells them that there is an objection to the winner – so don't give way to despair – and when they hear that their horse has now been declared the winner they leap around, sing out and hug each other.

They are told it is raining and they attempt to cover their heads, that it is sunny and warm and they pretend to sun-bathe. (It seemed to me that a dream was being enacted on that stage.) They sit down after all the excitement and are told they will all go off to sleep again and when they wake each one will take off his right shoe, nurse it and believe it to be a puppy, but they will laugh at the others who are nursing shoes. It is an odd spectacle to see a dozen adults, each cud-dling and stroking a shoe, at the same time laughing at others who are engaged in like antics. The hypnotist arouses them with a snap of his fingers, and now a hefty young chap takes on the name of his female neighbour on the stage, as she imagines herself a man. He powders up, lipstick and eye pencil – all mimed – to go out. The hypnotist suggests they are at the bar, pours water into glasses, tells them it is brandy, they drink it, appear to be drunk, and start singing songs. After an hour or more of the same, the performance draws to a close: 'You will be your normal selves when you go back to your places,' he tells them, after making them recover by a wave of the hand, 'but then you will each be a three-year-old, and sit on the knee of the person next to you.'

They trooped off stage as fresh and natural as they went on, and walked back to their places, but it was odd to see the young fellow in my row, clamber on to the lap of the man

THE DREAM MIND

next to him, curl up, knees under chin, and start sucking his thumb; similar behaviour was going on all over the place. Then a clap of the hands and a call from the hypnotist released them all from the spell. I chatted later to the man who imagined himself to be a woman. He was on holiday with his parents and girlfriend, and he told me he couldn't remember a thing. I also had a talk with a man who sat next to me: there was no question of any faking. (I do not know if it is so, yet despite all the absurd notions the hypnotist was able to suggest and have accepted, I imagine a hypnotist would fail to satisfy the thirst of a thirsty man or the hunger of a hungry one: as in a dream I feel sure this would only work if there was no actual thirst or hunger.)

From the extraordinary range of hypnotic phenomena I will stress one factor – the post-hypnotic directive which manifests itself when the subject appears to be no longer under hypnotic control. In the theatre the subjects got on the lap of the person beside then; in controlled experiments the subject may appear to be perfectly normal, yet later will follow instructions which were given under hypnosis, such as picking specks of dust off a carpet, imagining there is a fly around which he has to catch, or taking off his shoes. Something of a like nature, I am led to believe, occurs during dreaming. The power of the dream is more pervasive than we imagine, and any genuine attempt at oneirocriticism must tap the vein of interpretation predetermined in the dream itself. Every dreamer who has his own set theory about dreams, be it Freudian, Jungian or that of the Greco-Roman world, or of the Mohave or Iroquois Indians, or from Siberian Shamans or *Old Moore's Almanac*, will have it adumbrated in his dreams – with fairly clear hints as to how he should go about discovering the 'meaning' (dream suggestions never contradict the drift of the dreamer's psyche). This expedient engages those strands of conscious reason which float through dreams when sleep is light, harnessing them to the dream, thickening the dream web, and preventing extrinsic thought encroaching on the dream process – an intrusion which, as has been explained, would weaken the flow of the dream by exposing it to reason, which in turn might give rise to a scepticism as to the reality of the happenings. The Dream Mind knows exactly how to engage the imagination of the dreamer, since it is one with the very source of imagery; if at the same time it can seduce the intellect the clutch of the dream is strengthened.

# 11

# *The Disparate Twins*

*'Bear in mind that what pulls the strings is that Hidden
Thing within us: That makes our speech, That our life,
That, one may say, makes the man. Never in thy mental
picture of it include the vessel that overlies it, nor these
organs that are appurtenances thereof.'*

To apprehend fully what Marcus Aurelius was getting at,
and at the same time acquire a better understanding of the
dream function, we need to identify more clearly the intrinsic duality of our cognitive processes. Briefly, there is the
cerebral faculty, which exercises all volitional mental activity of a rational and discursive nature, memory, discrimination and judgement, which I shall call the Civilised Mind.
In contradistinction there is also the *Hidden Thing*, a subliminal or superconscious power, the fount of all imaginative
and creative activity, the Archemind or Superconscious. We
*think* – That *knows*. Mental action is not of the function of
the omniscient Archemind which in us is a wholly intuitive
one, such as the 'flash of inspiration' which is said to have

struck Archimedes in the bathtub, Newton under the apple tree, Fleming when he spotted the green mould of penicillin, and countless other discoverers. The Archemind is the senior intelligence, operating free of any reasoning, and capable of manipulating its conscious twin in most situations in which they clash. This we are naturally reluctant to accept – that human intelligence is not free and independent, but governed for biological ends. This covert determinant in our thought and behaviour, can serve as guide and prompter, but we need to be wary of its essential bias: 'From birth to death,' to quote Plato, 'the soul is bereft of reason against its will.'

The conditioning process by which we are often bereft of reason begins in infancy: up to around the age of five – this at least is my own belief – the child absorbs most impressions through the Archemind, in a totally self-centred manner. Attitudes established in those early years become fixed, a sort of psychical imprinting which, short of a conversion, is immutable. Religious fanaticism and bigotry, chauvinism and social discrimination, when instilled by upbringing, are there to stay. It would seem that each one of us creates his or her own cache of personal convictions, the more irrational the more strongly they take over. That which is not the product of reason will not be influenced by it. Perhaps it is not so much that the racist and fanatic behave in a dogmatic fashion, but that they have little choice – their trend of thought is directed for them. 'The mind having once acquired a bias is very ready to accept as evidence all that agrees with this,' wrote Virginia Woolf's doctor, 'and to reject what may be in opposition to the favourite idea.' We don't think, we are thought.

Throughout life, it would appear, that what is taken to be intelligence, that is the capacity to think and behave rationally, is allowed to comprehend only so much at each stage, ensuring that reason does not inhibit instinct, such as when falling in love. Few are those who can claim not to have made fools of themselves in this area at one time or another – that 'love subverts reason' is only too true; and it seems unlikely that reason and most sexual activity could operate simultaneously. Man, it would appear, has an innate tendency to break loose from the bonds of reason, and Nature connives in providing numerous fruits, flowers and fungi which yield drugs that beguile the senses.

It would seem that at some stage in human evolution, as the function of the brain increased – possibly around the period of *Homo erectus*, as once Man got on to his two legs he had to start thinking for himself – there appears to have developed a dichotomy, a splitting of what had been the single autochthonous intelligence. Reason and logic, being late concepts in man, their realisation must have superseded functions of instinct, the word displacing signs and howls as a form of communication, an alphabet making symbols redundant. However, since we have come to regard our conscious exercise of 'the mind' as the measure of all understanding, we naturally find it difficult to accept the idea of being inspired, guided, misguided, and generally kept on a rein by a superior, or at least a more powerful, intelligence – one immanent but clearly beyond human ingenuity to analyse. So limited is our awareness of the influences motivating our assumptions, our thinking and our actions as we go though life that it could be said that most of the time we are partly unconscious of what it is all about.

Dreaming is one instrument of this Power – and probably it is engendered in the womb, that first glimmering of the faculty of imagination. The cry of the newborn infant, sometimes evoked by a slap, is probably the shock of being woken from a deep dream, one which has held it for months (it certainly sounds like that). And it is odd how even the youngest baby appears to know what fear is, despite the most sheltered life and loving parents. Antenatal dreaming could also be a rehearsal for lactation; the assured way in which the newborn child makes for the mother's breast, an instinctive reflex action, perhaps taught by the dream.

Much respect is paid to reason as a guiding principle of human behaviour, but we seem eager to set it aside when the occasion suits; this deviation occurs during any activity associated with war, and will swiftly derange an otherwise sane people. There are those in whose lives reason plays almost no part – likes and dislikes serving better. In a personal relationship the dogmatic partner will get the better of the reasonable one – nor will intelligence triumph over stubbornness, since it lacks the drive. In finance and business it would seem that ambition, cupidity, cunning and thrust easily outstrip reason and intelligence. As for politics, on scanning the world history it is manifestly obvious, judging from certain of the most influential figures of this century, reason and wisdom make a poor showing against egotism, demagoguery and the knack of being able to dupe others.

## 12

# *Extrasensory Perception*

The well-known Maury 'Guillotine Dream' may hint at extrasensory perception operating during sleep. Maury, when young, had been reading about the French revolution during an illness, the scenes making a deep impression on him; he dreamt he was involved in the Reign of Terror, witnessing scenes of murder, being questioned himself, and he was led to the place of execution, with the mob clamouring all around. Next he was bound prone to the plank, the cord was pulled and the heavy blade fell upon his neck and his head was cleaved from his body. He woke up to find that the top of the bed had fallen down, and had apparently struck him in the same place as the executioner's blade in the dream.

The inference of this at the time – which was taken up by journalists and others, became generally accepted, and even persists to the present day in certain minds – was that as the collapse of the bed-post could not have been anticipated, then the entire dream which led up to it must have taken place in the brief moments between the post striking Maury and his awakening; this, it was said, would have accounted for the shock which woke him up. Freud explains the rapidity of thought by suggesting the possibility that Maury's dream represented a fantasy that had been stored up in the memory, and which was alluded to at the precise moment he was struck by the bed-post, and presumably issued forth in a flash; he suggests it could have had its source in the attraction of Maury imagining himself as an aristocrat and bravely mounting the scaffold, or even that of being the 'heroic Danton', and by this Freud postulates the Maury dream as one of wish fulfilment. It is difficult to credit the number of fanciful theories to which that dream gave rise. One put forward by Edward Goblot, a French logician, that a dream occupies only the time it takes for us to awake – 'A dream is an awakening that is a beginning' – Freud believed to be an interesting concept.

I would anatomise Maury's dream in the understanding that sleep is clearly not the complete split from waking life into an unknowing mental state which it would appear to be – this we can confirm from the ECG patterns. 'The great gift of sleep' is its own autonomous condition, a state in some way even more vital to life than wakefulness, judging from how long we may survive without it; there is much to suggest that it may have preceded consciousness, which could have been a later development. Our imaginative powers are surely at their peak during dreaming, and there are other faculties that sleep would appear to assume. This is indicated in the manner in which we often resolve before going to sleep to awake at a certain hour – and how this usually, if not invariably, happens. I know of persons who claim that they can wake up to the minute they choose, even though they change the waking hour; all they need to do, apparently, is to state clearly as they give a final look at the clock what time they wish to wake up. 'I've got a waking-up system that works very well' – I quote from a newspaper interview with a successful businessman, 'I normally get up at 6 a.m., but I can say to myself, for example, "3.28 a.m.", and that's when I wake up.' Kleitman gives awaking experiments made by an investigator, Frobenius, where five subjects were tested on 250 nights, and it was demonstrated that they were able to wake up within five minutes of the time set for them. In sleep it is clear that there are various latent factors at work, of which we have no conscious awareness.

I can usually rely upon waking up when I need to – but as I am a light sleeper I cannot vouch with certainty of the power. However, I will give one dream example from many, of the need to rise at a certain hour. I had risen one morning at four o'clock, ate a light breakfast, then wrote and read, and around half-past seven went back to bed, warning myself that I had an appointment and must be up by nine o'clock. I went off to sleep fairly soon and concluded a spell of dreaming with the following:

*Dream*: I had gone to an ironmonger's shop to buy a torch. Joe, the assistant, kept messing around with a naked light, in amongst the shelves, and I had an impulse to warn him of the danger, but since he was a chap who didn't like advice I thought better of it. Twice he nearly set the place alight, but we managed to put out the flames. Yet again he went into a corner, and accidentally set a fire going. The boss turned up and attempted to put it out, and so did Joe, then I jumped on a chair and called out for buckets of water to dowse it, but there was no water and it grew hotter and I had to jump down to escape.

I woke up, and to my surprise found that I was comfortable in bed, no heat, no discomfort, with a pleasant breeze coming in the open window. Odd that I should have had such an alarming dream, I thought, as I rested back, ready to doze off again. Suddenly it struck me that I should be up at nine. I got up in some alarm, looked at the clock, and saw it was five minutes past nine. My goodness, I thought, that must have been why I woke up. The odd thing was that as I was dressing it seemed that this same intuition was prompting me what to do, what to wear and much else. Not only are we guided in sleep, but throughout our waking hours a superior Intelligence will nudge us along – if only we learn to heed its intimations.

The Dream Mind seems to be aware of certain physical phenomena within a prescribed radius – even to the point of apparent precognition. I have always had a dislike of being startled awake by an alarm clock, and would always wake up moments before one went off, allowing me time to switch the alarm off; the same has also been true of occasions when I have arranged for a telephone call to waken me. The state of unconsciousness during the deepest sleep is not total in the sense we imagine it to be; instinct can and does exercise itself and stir into low-keyed action the apparently dormant senses. Take for example the phenomenon of sleepwalking: Kleitman tells of an attested case of a family of somnambulists (father and mother cousins, with four children) who got up at three o'clock in the morning, all fast asleep, grouped round the tea table in the kitchen, and were awakened only by the sharp sound when one of them upset a chair. In certain experiments pans of cold water were placed round a bed, but some of the sleepwalkers learned how to avoid them, even though they were asleep. There is a report of a man sleepwalking along the ledge of a building on the twelfth storey, and going back to bed without waking. A student was known to get up and regularly go off for a swim without having any later recollection of it. And I have spoken to a boy of ten who told me how he must have got up one night, gone to the fridge, and eaten a full plate of smoked salmon which had been prepared for a party next day: 'At least,' he said, 'that's what they told me I'd done.'

Now back to the Maury dream – I believe that an awareness of the loose bed-post was registered by the Dream Mind; moreover, it is probable that the youthful Maury heard some creak or other before going off to sleep (bed-posts rarely collapse instantly) without giving it a second thought. We must also take into account that he was ill and feverish – a state when sleep is normally inhibited because of the dangers to the sleeping person, and no doubt he was in need of sleep. On his mind were scenes from the French revolution, which served as the medium to animate the dream. It was closely monitored from start to finish, the wild and tumultuous happenings rising and falling in accord with Maury's feverish condition ('I never dream really bright dreams,' Ruskin tells us, 'unless I'm ill'). The execution was repeatedly put off, and this would have continued, even with Maury waiting for the blow, had the bed-post not fallen when it did. If the post had remained intact the course of the dream would have been protracted but in that final instant as the bed-post was falling upon him the Dream Mind, in keeping with its cause-and-effect pattern, produced a dream reason for the impact. Had Maury not woken up the dream would have continued with him apparently headless. Decapitation is a fairly common dream device: 'Last night I dreamt that a Japanese man had a twin wire with which he was about to cut off my head,' a woman told me. '"It won't hurt," he said, "in fact you'll hardly feel it – " and with that he cut it off. I saw it lying there on the lawn, and I said to the gardener, "Don't you think we should bury it out of the way?"' Readers may interpret the dream as they wish – my own assumption would be that she no longer found her face as attractive as it had once been, and also that she was a very tidy woman. In which case both feelings were given expression in the dream.

## 13

## *Visual Stratagems*

The aesthetic pleasure experienced in certain dreams has often enchanted me over the years, yet it is seldom discussed, possibly because those who have not experienced it would find it difficult to conceive. It is most brilliantly realised in lucid dreams, but I have had a few dreams which seemed aimed at giving me, the dreamer, pure pleasure. I had one such dream in vivid colour, of a most attractive young woman leading me, her right arm around me, through a beautiful old town of Tudor houses. The sight delighted me, the feeling enriched by her youthful presence, as she tells me that her one wish, together with that of hoping to become an actress, is to have five pounds a week. You shall certainly have that, I tell her, but we shall have to see about your career. Such charming dreams come to me only when I am feeling very fit, or enjoying the euphoria that may accompany a recovery from illness – the dream is attuned to how one feels. Sometimes this sense of well-being produces gliding dreams, enhanced by some visual beauty, but touched with an exciting sense of danger, as in the following dream.

I am somewhere near the coast, with one of the young Scots fellows I used to play football with in Hyde Park – two happy associations: 'Come here, Bill,' he calls, as he manipulates the ropes of a huge hot-air balloon, ' – hold on to this,' and he gives me a rope to hold. I hold the rope while he adjusts the gear, then I get into the basket below, and the next thing we go off and are soon high up in the air. Rising up in the balloon is a most pleasant sensation, and looking away down I can see three young men who are bathers; one has dived into the sea at a loch, and is swimming down through the clear water, down deep to a rock at the bottom of the sea, and I watch the others dive into the sea and follow. It is an experience alive with beauty and excitement, and now I look about me, and see that we are very high up, and the thought crosses my mind that if anything goes wrong it will be certain death. I am about to speak to the Scots youth, intending to say, Do go careful! – but a warning idea crosses my mind: You might put him off. So I keep silent. Anyway, I must not show that I am afraid, I think, just leave myself in God's hands, as it were. The next thing we glide down towards earth. I am uneasy about how hard we may strike the ground, for we appear to be going very fast, but then he tells me we are already on the ground, standing beside the water. (This was the feeling I had a short time before when I went to have a cyst removed from my back, and was apprehensively waiting to feel the instrument, when I was told it was over and done.)

I woke up. I was feeling very fit; the previous evening visitors had called and I had drunk some champagne; during the day when walking along the beach I had been struck by the sight of a boy flying a kite that was very high up, which he made swing downwards and go up again, and I watched this for some time. But it struck me that had the dream been a film there would have been some clever camera work in the long and medium shots.

Sensation is usually a condition most likely to harmonise with sleep, since it fits so readily into the dreaming experience. Thought does not blend with dreaming, being a counter activity. A feeling of physical weariness is a sensation of sorts, and will usually help one to go to sleep; mental weariness will not help, the imaginative power required for dreaming being depleted. In the following dream there were some deft close-up shots.

*Dream*: I am in France, looking into a small shop window, where among miscellaneous articles there are some birthday cards. There is a crush around the window, and three French women are near me, one who is fairly young and looks rather like a Chinese woman; I start faking an interest in the cards, and listen as she reads out in broken English the messages on them. Inside the shop are a number of people, and I can see a man watching me closely, but I studiously ignore his gaze, and pretend an intense interest in the various cards, which I hold in my hands and inspect closely. I have a sense of being in a tightly framed scene, not unlike one from a film, the drama thickened by the three women close to me, and my awareness of the man watching. A noise woke me up.

A most dramatic visual effect as created in the following dream: I have gone to Victoria Station to see off a friend called

Brenda, but have become parted from her. I am anxious, nervous and disquieted, but must continue to hang around looking for Brenda. The part of Victoria Station where I am is separated from the departing area by a huge wall, but there is a television screen with pictures of all that is happening on the runway (the railway station has become an airport). The television screen by use of selection gives a clear and telling picture of all that is happening on the vast airfield. I find I am deeply involved in the scene around me, for I am watching for Brenda among the people milling about, and at the same time by glancing at the television screen I can see the planes leaving. Suddenly I see what appears to be a rocket, rising up from amongst the planes, the nose of the rocket having a fiery appearance, and then I hear a low sinister explosion. My God, I think, the plane is on fire! (The report of a plane crash at Malaga, which plane then caught fire, had been on the news that week and the thought of the dead and injured had stuck in my mind.) I see on the television screen the fire from the airfield spreading rapidly, and coming towards the station. The next moment the flames are rising above the walls and the station walls are crashing down. Oh God, to think that my wife is only a mile away, I say to myself, waiting in the flat, and will never know I was here – and I shall be killed or burnt to death! The people are now rushing around wildly, and there is heat and smoke and no way of getting out. Oh my god, I pray, if this is to be my end let it be my end. The walls come crashing down and the flames draw nearer. I woke up.

In certain dreams a bizarre note will be introduced to catch the dreamer's interest, should it be flagging. I dream I have gone to a public swim bath like the one I knew in Bolton as a boy, and first I make to the foot-bath to wash down, but find I cannot get in because men are lying around in the water half asleep, and one chap is lying there wearing all his clothes and his big dirty boots. The scene caught my interest at once, but also kept me out of the water.

Towards the end of another dream I am talking to an Italian café proprietor, telling him about a criminal the police are after who has the nickname of Little Joe, and who has never been caught, when suddenly I exclaim, 'Why here he is!' I have just spotted a Lilliputian figure on the pavement, not more than six inches high, and I bend down to pick him up. It seems that I know of a mixture, one of port and some-thing else that would bring him back to normal, but I find I haven't time to prepare it, as I feel a need to go to the toilet. I woke up, and found I had the need, but felt it was a shrewd if unsuccessful attempt to keep me sleeping. The opposite visual effect can also serve.

I dream I am on a visit to Bolton on a Saturday evening, and am going along a familiar street where I often walked when I was a boy. There are a number of young men there I know and I am friendly with, but the tallest of all is very well over nine feet. 'Isn't that Brian?' I ask, and I am told it is. Brian nods to me, a bit ashamedly, I feel, from his great height. I recall how I had recently heard of his death, and I remember that his long neck made him seem taller than he was. This must nearly be seen as being dead, I think to myself, as Brian stoops down to shake hands with me. End of dream. Such happenings in dreams are shock effects, easy to achieve, for they are purely visual, and entail little imaginative activity.

The following dream illustrates the conflict between the Dream Mind in striving to keep the dreamer asleep against the activity of senses, which would awaken him. I was almost asleep but not quite – in a state of half dreaming. It was early morning, my wife had gone into the bathroom, and the sound of her washing and dressing – with the bathroom adjacent to the wall where our beds were set – was keeping me from going off fully to sleep. I was dreaming of planting shrubs – a task which I had planned for myself during the night. The dream images seemed to be closer and larger and more intense than normal – probably a heightened form of dreaming to pull me more deeply into sleep. Suddenly there was a loud sharp sound as the bathroom door was pulled open by my wife. At that moment the shrub, now very close up in the dream, was cut right through, and all I saw was a thick bunch of stem-like growths all cut off. It was a most vivid image, and as I say, brought to a giant close-up to me for heightened effect – a device the Dream Mind uses when necessary – and was presented as being the consequence of the action of cutting, implied by the door sound. If my wife had not spoken to me, and made more sound when she came into the bedroom, that dream image may have drawn me back into sleep. (Jung tells of how he was once falling off to sleep and had a vision of a large fish, and just as he lost consciousness the wardrobe gave a loud crack and he opened his eyes to see a large fish emerging from the top corner – which phenomenon he relates to the 'exteriorised libido'. I would suggest it was a startling dream image, produced to divert his mind from the sound and to lure him back to sleep and dreaming.)

# 14

## *The Dead in Dreams*

Freud quotes the following as examples of what he regards as the misconceptions of various scientists and philosophers about dreams: 'There are no dreams that are absolutely reasonable, and that do not contain *some* incoherence, anachronism or absurdity', and 'A dream is psychical, emotional and mental anarchy'. I should be inclined to agree, except that anarchy implies an ungoverned activity, whereas dreaming is a tightly governed function, outside the criteria of reason. Others stated: 'There is no imaginable thing too absurd, too involved, or too abnormal for us to dream about it' and 'The content of at least nine out of ten dreams is nonsensical.' Those comments are obvious enough, but surely the interesting fact about dreams is that they work, and no matter how absurd they are the dreamer believes them as he is dreaming – which is all that matters. A non-reasoning factor in our behaviour need not signify a defective agency, but a necessary negation of reason. 'The wise part of us,' Amiel writes, 'is that which is unconscious of itself; and what is most reasonable in a man are those elements in him which do not reason.' Reason and meaning are concepts of civilisation, not of Nature; in dreaming, which is a purely imaginational experience, they have no place.

The ambiguity of such terms as Freud's 'the Unconscious' and Jung's 'Collective Unconscious' gives rise to the impression of a secondary intelligence; we need to see it as 'the Superconscious', a power that not only colours our thought but regulates it. In making reference to the dead appearing in dreams our two authorities appear to ascribe a significance where I would suggest that none exists. I see no distinction between 'quick and the dead' in my own dreams, where they mingle freely, and all are quick. How could we dream of our many deceased relatives and friends, and chat away to them unaware of any incongruity, if there existed a dream difference between the living and the dead? The only occasion when the fact of a dream character being dead has an implication, and this an inapt one, is when the death of the person, and events associated with it, have had a keen emotional effect upon the dreamer, leaving an impression of death that for a time eclipses that of the living person. The consequence of this is that a character who is *physically* dead to the dreamer many turn up in dreams.

Among such dreams of my own was one about a neighbour called Tom, a big man of forceful character, who was suddenly to learn of his having a malignant tumour. We had often argued over the garden fence – he was unashamedly racist and right-wing in his views – and I later visited him daily during his illness, witnessed his rapid decline, and finally my wife and I were called into the home minutes after he had died. He was seated up in bed, his eyes open, but I watched as my wife, a nurse, put him lying down straight, closed his eyes and put pads of damp cotton wool over them. I saw this once robust man, now cold and grey, stiffening in rigor mortis, and the sight made a deep impression on me – intimating more vividly than I could have imagined my own demise. Some months after his death I had a dream in which he turned up at a party: Tom, I thought, this can't be real! But from his look I could see that Tom was aware of what my dreaming self was thinking, and to contradict my thought he began to laugh and joke loudly and fling himself defiantly around in lively dance. My mother was at the party (she had been dead for thirty years) and I whispered to her, 'But he's dead, Mother – God rest him.' 'Oh he'll recover,' she said. The dream went on, and I tried to keep to my own impression, but it seemed that Tom was out to prove I was wrong, and he grinned at me, stared me out, and danced on, as though to dispel both my memory and reason – which in the dream he partly succeeded.

*How can he dance when I know he is dead?* was the thought that crossed my mind. Such a contretemps sidetracks the dream and must be swiftly resolved, one way or another. Freud tells of a dream in which he and his friend Fleiss are in conversation with a deceased friend named Paneth, whom Freud is aware of being dead. They go to some place where they sit and talk; Paneth fails to understand something that Fleiss tells him, and Fleiss turns to ask Freud how much he had told Paneth about his affairs. Freud feels overcome by strange emotions, and tries to explain that Paneth could not understand anything, because he was not alive. 'I then gave Paneth a piercing look,' he writes. 'Under my gaze he turned pale; his form grew indistinct and his eyes a sickly blue – and he finally melted away.' It seemed wholly in character for the redoubtable Freud to dispatch the misfit Paneth by that powerful gaze, much different from my own dream quandary in which I was outdone by the deceased.

Dream characters whom we recognise as being dead are seldom those we have lived with over our most impressionable years, but those we have known less intimately, whose death we have had particular cause to remember. The memories we have of someone much loved – or, it must be said, possibly hated or feared – stretching over the years, are so implanted as to ensure a rich source of dream material; as the memory of the brief period from death to interment fades away, the more fixed memories revive, obliterating others. It hardly needs pointing out that a child who has feared his father, and has often dreamt of him in later years, will not cease to have such dreams of him once the father is dead. Were the fact of death to change such characters, or eliminate them from our dreams, our stock of dream figures would soon be depleted – especially so in old age. To attempt to differentiate between those characters of our dreams who are actually living or dead would be like doing so when watching an old movie; or believing a novelist should make a like distinction – to use only living prototypes and reject the dead.

My brother-in-law, Bert, was a good friend, but after my moving to London we rarely met, and I was saddened when I heard of his early death, returned for his funeral, and saw him lying in his coffin, and was involved in the funeral arrangements. It was years later I dreamt I was in a theatre watching some men playing a game that was a mixture of golf and billiards. After a time, and to my amazement, I recognised one of the players as Bert. But surely he can't be alive, came a dream thought, for I clearly remember his funeral twenty years ago. Yet no doubt but that it was Bert, and he looked as young as when I had first known him. I decided I must go and speak to him – I never imagined I was dreaming, of course – and when the game was over I made my way to him: 'Bert,' I said, 'it's me – Bill!' At once his face changed into that of a much older man, hardly at all like what had been his remembered self. He seemed embarrassed, and then explained to me that yes, he was Bert, and that he had come back to earth to help out an old mate of his who was in trouble. He had been waiting for someone to tell him to go back – apparently he couldn't return until he had been recognised – and now that I had spoken to him he could go. Then my sister May – also long departed – turned up, and as so often happened in the old days we went off together, then came to a large lift into which they both went. The lift doors closed, and I thought Bert looked rather uncertain and unhappy, but as I saw them both moving upward the feeling I had was that it would be all right. I woke up.

The explanation is simple enough: over the years preceding his death I had rarely met Bert, and then it was his corpse I looked down at. Following this I was to find myself comforting my sister, piling up wreaths, being one of the coffin-bearers into my old church for Requiem Mass, and later scattering earth on his coffin. This emotive experience of his interment overlaid my memory of his living self, and asserted itself during the dream. The bare news of the death of someone dear to us, without some witness of the fact, does not impress itself on us at once – and without the keen funeral impression the memory would not have intervened, and probably I should have joined Bert in the game myself, as may have been intended.

Often the heart will not easily accept that a loved one is dead – many mothers refuse to believe that a son has been killed in war – and for the death of someone most dear to occupy our psychic awareness it appears to need a ritual of sorts. Today many close relatives, even a husband or a wife, prefer not to see the dead person, the stiff upper lip often suppressing tears. Irish wakes, with the dead one lying shrouded and silent, amidst all the drinking and smoking of pipes, followed by keening at the funeral, created a memorable image of the person as dead, one which expunged that of his being alive.

What I took to be a neat resolution of a dreamer's awareness of a dream character being dead, yet with the Dream Mind having a need to employ the character in some further capacity in the dream, was a dream a woman told me which occurred shortly after the death of her father, whose funeral she had recently attended. He had been a stern, Calvinistic figure of whom she had always gone in fear, and in the dream she was in the family coach behind the cortège as it approached the cemetery. But there was an unexpected setback – the gates were locked against them, because of a strike by cemetery workers. Pickets were lined up outside to see that no funeral party got in, and this obstruction created much distress among the mourners, aggravated by the fact that there was nothing anyone could do about it. Then just as they were all about to turn back, the coffin lid was seen to open, and out stepped her father, got the key, ordered them to one side, unlocked and opened the gates, directed the procession through, then halted it whilst he got back into his coffin, closed down the lid, and the funeral continued. What particularly struck her in the dream, she said, was the feeling that it was all so much in character with her father, who would not allow anything to stand in his way.

# 15

## *Dream Stimuli*

Our interrupted reflections, unexpressed thoughts, failed intentions, frustrated desires – any one of these emotive snippets will be stored away by the Dream Mind, until at some dream contingency the appropriate one will turn up, transformed beyond recognition, to catch our interest. A song that I liked when young was 'The Last Rose of Summer', but the tune seemed to elude me, so that when I heard a woman's voice singing it in a dream I was enchanted. Then I woke up, and as I lay there in the darkness thinking over the song, I became aware of a hinge in the open window creaking from a sudden breeze, and somewhat reluctantly was forced to identify that particular dream mimicry. In another dream I was in an operating theatre, with surgeons about to operate on me, and this it later transpired had diverted my attention from a pain in the stomach.

On a number of occasions I have had dreams of making journeys in my bare feet, walking up grassy hills, stepping along wet streets, or even gardening in my bare feet, then after some minutes of being awake – one does not take note of it at once – I have found that my feet have poked out from between the bedclothes and are cold. Stroke a sleeping person on the ear with a feather, or on the nose, and you will get a corresponding dream reaction – providing he or she is one who recalls dreams, and is awakened shortly after; dip the feather in cold water and put to the sleeping forehead and this again will be simulated in the dream. Often the stimulus is not recognised, and it was only after I had a number of dreams of playing football in Hyde Park that I became aware that these always occurred when the electric fan was running, and in the darkness I realised that the sound was almost identical to that of the drone of the nearby Park Lane traffic that was always heard during the pauses on the football field. A sleeper subjected to sound during sleep will dream of a situation in which this may be part of the background, or make a central dream situation.

Dreaming can absorb a considerable degree of sound, providing the source is not too close to the sleeper and the crescendo is gradual – which allows for a dream simulation to be set up; but a much quieter sound, such as a spoon dropping on the floor, will waken the sleeper, since the sound cannot be intercepted. Conversely, the dream which is simulating sound cannot absorb a silence. For example, should an infant go to sleep to the loud whining of a vacuum cleaner, and the cleaner is suddenly shut off, it will waken up – the sudden silence being difficult to assimilate into a dream situation.

I dreamt I was working in a factory, when a substance like snow got on my skin and after some time began causing irritation. I woke up, thought about the dream, and realised it was a memory of my youth, when I had a job at a mercerising works that entailed using caustic soda, causing an intense stinging of the skin on both hands and feet; I also became aware that I was actually suffering from an irritant caused by an excess of chlorine in the water of a swim pool. The mercerising works was a vast, open and unheated place, wet and draughty, and during the winters I often suffered from tonsillitis; sixty years later a sore throat will bring up dreams of the works and the period.

My first job on leaving school was in a weaving shed, with a dusty atmosphere, and tiny particles of dust often got in my eyes. Fifty years later I went to bed one night aware of a speck of lint in my eye, and all night long I dreamt of the weaving shed. When in my twenties I started filling and carrying bags of coal for a living, working in the open air and enjoying three good sweats daily, I became exceptionally fit and strong. Some twenty years later – after a few years of sedentary habits as a writer – I started playing football and jogging, and there was a revival of the sweating I had once known, so that I again took on the earlier feeling of a robust fitness, which seems to go with sweating of that kind, and I found that many dreams brought up the coal-filling job. Health is only one of the various associations with past periods of life which come up in dreams, and that can be traced back by the dreamer alone. When a healthy and contented person is sleeping peacefully, the Dream Mind must set up a felicitous counterworld of dreaming, since the two states, that of the sleeper and that of the dream, must harmonise. In such situations I find that the characters in my dreams are those usually associated with happy times, and friends whose company I loved.

An improbable stimulus was spotted at the end of the following dream: I am in a doctor's surgery close to a woman doctor who has an attractive face, and a wide mouth with large well-spaced teeth. Her face comes close to mine as she takes my blood pressure, simply by putting a matchstick under my armpit. As she explains the new procedure in a clear voice I find myself looking at her teeth, and recalling how as a boy I had been impressed on learning that teeth with spaces between were the best kind. During this close gaze at her wide mouth and white teeth I woke up. It was early morning, and after some moments, when looking towards the drawn curtains at the window, I noticed the bright morning light had penetrated below the pelmet, creating a horizontal shaft of light, to which the white vertical splits in the dark room gave the appearance of a huge mouth with spaced teeth. I am most sensitive to light, and slowly I realised that such clear light would have woken me earlier had not the dream simulated it into that mouth with white teeth. An association was that of having had my blood pressure taken the day before by a woman doctor, during which the thought had crossed my mind that the sphygmomanometer seemed an old-fashioned instrument for modern medical practice, and that there was a fortune for anyone who could invent a gadget to replace it.

It is reassuring to find certain of my own dream findings are confirmed and often from an unexpected quarter. In *The Discovery of the Unconscious* by Henri F. Ellenberger, I came across an account of associations of a more urbane variety, recounted by the Marquis Hervey de Saint-Denis (1922–1892), who made a lifelong study of his own dreams. Over a period of twenty years he wrote down every dream he had (I would say *recalled*), the following being two of his associative dream experiments. During a fortnight stay away from Paris – Hervey taught Chinese at the Collège de France – when he was in the countryside at Vivarais, he put a drop of a certain perfume on his handkerchief every day. He ceased to do so on his return to Paris, but several months later arranged that on some unspecified night in the future, his assistant, unknown to Hervey, should put drops of the same perfume on the pillow whilst Hervey was asleep. Twelve nights later Hervey dreamt of Vivarais, and on awakening realised that the perfume had been put on his pillow that same night. Another experiment was at a ball; Hervey arranged with the musicians that when he danced with one of his two partners they should play a certain tune, and when he danced with the other lady they were to play another tune. Later, he had the tunes played on a music box whilst he was asleep, and on each occasion, Hervey tells us, the tune played brought up in his dreams the particular partner.

I should imagine that in Hervey's case the associated stimuli alone did not evoke the dreams, but that a certain anticipative autosuggestion was also at work. Ellenberg remarks that Hervey 'knew how to provoke frequent and abundant dreams', but I believe this to be mistaken. What Hervey learnt – and I take it to be similar to my own dream experience – was how to cultivate a certain watchfulness during sleep, which served both to magnify and clarify the incessant dream flow; the dreams he recalled were those which a period of wakefulness, no matter how brief, enabled him to impress on his memory. Most of the earlier flow of dreaming must have eluded him, as it does us all, unless we are suddenly aroused.

# 16

## *Daily Dream Drama*

It usually happens that on our waking in the morning, taking a shower or bath, dressing and setting about our daily tasks, all memory of our dreams vanishes except for the odd trace. However the innate dream instinct – for such I am convinced it is – does not remain wholly dormant until we go to sleep again; apart from spells of daydreaming, the instinct likes to be fed. The media have a ready supply, of a kind that may titillate and excite and can be wholly forgotten – as happens with a dream. The fascination exerted by radio and television, and the daily perusal of newspapers splashed with headlines, accompanied by pictures and comic strips, lies in the fact of such being vicarious forms of conscious dream sensation. The variety of approaches to the ritual of that first tasting of the morning newspaper can be observed any weekday – from the businessman in the train to the motor mechanic grabbing a few minutes over his tea break. There is a basic similarity in performance of them all, indicated by what would appear to be a need to escape the stress of self-generated thought, and divert the imagination with a readymade packet of miscellaneous happenings, a joke or two, and the tasting of a dozen or more varied episodes in as many minutes. A greedy reader cannot bear to put off his first glimpse at his newspaper, and will turn to it at once, strolling along a busy street or railway platform. When he gets settled down with it he turns eagerly from one page to another, darts from item to item, from picture to cartoon and comic strip, and the more exciting the news, the more graphic the images, the more he is gripped – just as in a dream.

Good news will not sell newspapers, it rarely fuels the imagination; the news of a man reaching the moon will sell them, but only for the first time or two, but a man or a dog missing on the moon or on a rocket and disappearing into space will sell more. Human curiosity, the 'what will happen next?' factor – as in dreaming – allied to suspense, is what counts most: the trapped miners, missing mountaineers, a child down a manhole, even whales cut off from the ocean by an ice flow. In the absence of such dramatic events, news of royalty, prime ministers and presidents, film stars and pop singers will serve. A topic no newspaper can afford to neglect is that of human beings at play – in short, *sport*.

(This instinct for play, shared by all mammalian life from kittens, puppies, seals and on to whales, may well be associated with the make-believe of dreaming.) Then as the morning train draws into Charing Cross or wherever, or the work whistle blows, the reading expression gives way to the persona, in the manner of a sleeper being woken up, the newspaper is thrust aside and a new attitude is struck; the mechanic turns to the car engine and switches on his transistor radio. Should the newspaper habit be interrupted by a strike there is a sense of deprivement, followed by one of relief, and finally when the strike is over a disinclination to start all over again. Most readers prefer the same newspaper, written up in a style and spirit sympathetic to them, and a familiar format – only at peril may that affront to habituation be changed. Good advertising should always blend with the tone of the newspaper.

Touching on this dream instinct is the tendency of the natural mind to resist learning. A child will look at television for hours, read comic papers, listen to stories, but will usually avoid something being imparted which has to be *learned*, and consciously remembered – unless the pill is coated. That is the indulgent aspect of dreams – they are fed to us and then forgotten. In certain industrial societies which are tightly organised the people may become starved of their daily dream substitute, signs of which can often be seen in the fixed expression on their faces. Conversely, when there is little direction of thought, with too much watching of television, there comes a besotted look, occasionally seen on the child or the young adult. A person who surrenders himself entirely to sleep, and who dreams perhaps a dozen hours a day, takes on that same befuddled look of one whose imagination has been sated.

The universal popularity of the novel indicates a certain voracious dream appetite. Almost all the well-known novels have proved suitable for filming; a novel that does not allow itself to be 'dreamt' will not prove compulsive reading. A volume of even the best short stories will attract fewer readers than a mediocre novel, one with plenty of action and suspense, because with stories the reader has to stop and start again, discard one mood and take up another – no dream that went on like that would succeed. 'I'm a greedy reader,' a friend told me, 'and when I'm not too busy and can let myself go I'll read about six books in a week. However, which may not sound very flattering to you as an author, I forget the name of any author, or indeed much of the book, and must admit that I can seldom recall anything I've read.' This form of reading is clearly one of dream substitution. Reading of that kind is a process of evoking a series of images, held vaguely in mind for a short time, scarcely making any impression on the memory itself, and then being dispelled from mind like a dream. Another aspect of dreaming engaged upon during such reading is the shutting out of external reality. People with many worries will often turn to reading as an escape from immediate problems – about which they may feel they can do little of a positive value anyway. Unhappy children, adults too, will often sleep for long periods.

There are various forms of reading, but two main kinds: reading wholly by mind and reading by imagination (there is also, in reading poetry, a fusing of the two, but we need not pursue that here). Reading by mind is a form of studying, applying oneself and attempting to register all that one is reading; this is seldom a pleasure, and is not fuelled by the impulse of the Dream Mind. Reading by imagination is reading purely for pleasure, all can be forgotten once the newspaper or book has been put down. The reading of fiction is not only a form of dream sensation, but a novel when recalled will often appear to be a memory of a dream.

# 17

## *Idiosyncratic Dreams*

Any impression I may have given of all my dreams being first-class I must dispel at once, since I have had hundreds of dreams I thought were simply not worth the trouble of writing down. Dreaming I find to be far from a standard performance, in which every dream implements its function perfectly. Dreams might be judged like films, with points for criteria such as plot, action and dialogue, and above all the power to enthrall. There are well-structured dreams, with a beginning, a middle and an end that all relate, and there are makeshift dreams, seemingly cobbled together, lacking form and continuity, dreams which start off with one theme and switch to another, lose a character or two along the way, and introduce extraneous ones. The reasons are manifold, from the fact that there are minds which are skilful weavers of dreams and others that are clumsy botchers. The former are usually possessed of a fertile imagination, whilst the dream botchers are those who are less gifted in the area of the imagination.

Just as there are periods of what is called 'creativity' in a writer's life, there are others in which the imagination seems inert, so would it appear to be with our dream life. Then the dreams are presented unevenly, the images blurred, as though all were not right in the operator's box as well. There are even some boring dreams – as reluctant as I am to admit such – and also dreams that are simply distasteful. I had a sequence of such dreams one night – I woke up a number of times, but the situation remained largely the same, one in which I have the job of gutting and cleaning fish, and packing them into boxes. As I do not care much for fish, seldom eat it from choice, and dislike the smell, the dreams were no more than disagreeable. Even so, I finally decided it was preferable to lie awake, which I did after getting up for a short time.

The fancies, feelings and stimuli that need to be absorbed in our dreams are often so varied and diverse, with bodily upset, sexual urge, inner tensions and external disturbances of sound and movement, creating a discordant jumble which impedes the normal unifying dream process, that in place of a sequential flow we get grotesque and conflicting episodes. Kafka tells of such in his diary: '… plagued by dreams, as if they were being scratched on me, a stubborn material.' One night I could hear a violent storm outside my bedroom window, and after having been awake for a long time I finally fell asleep, and had the following dream: I am at home in the late evening, lying on my bed, alone and aware of erotic inclinations, which I promise myself I shall indulge when my wife gets home. Finally, after some ill-humoured waiting on my part, she arrives, but from where I am lying on the bed I see a number of women visitors following her in. The disconcertment I feel, together with a sense of frustration and annoyance, is made worse by the fact that the visitors, five of them, are all black women, slim and tall with long narrow faces, and at once I feel an obligation to avoid the least show of ill-grace. But clearly they don't feel the same restraint, for as they prepare to make their beds on the floor beside mine, one calls out in a bossy manner for me to take off her shoes. I get out of bed, go down on my knees and start struggling to take off her shoes, which I manage only with much difficulty. My temper has now risen, and gets the better of me, and I turn on my wife, shout at her, and at the same time start slapping her. Yet as I do so I keep telling myself to stop – that I'll be so sorry later for what I am doing. Suddenly I realise it is not my wife I am slapping but one of the guests, and I apologise profusely to her; then a man just like myself, but a much younger self, stands up in front of me, and at once I start kicking him. Then I call to my wife: 'This is only a dream – have everything right for me when I wake up.' I do not wake instantly, but pray, 'Oh God help me! God help me! God help me!'

I then wake up at once. I find I am overheated, my head and body tingling, and I have to take off my flannel pyjamas and lie naked to cool off, the storm raging outside, with sounds of gale and heavy rain. All this may have contributed to the turmoil and aggravated my overheated condition. As for my black guests, during the previous evening I had seen a picture of a sculptured bronze head, Nigerian, twelfth century, which had impressed me; later, I read of the people of Somalia, with their straight noses and delicate features, and it had seemed curious to me that the Somali language, which is rich and poetic, was not written, no script for it was generally available, the official language and all the newspapers being in foreign tongues.

A dream will often provide the suspense or unease simply by some incongruous feature of the dream situation – one which for some reason has to be accepted. Some years ago on holiday my wife was almost the only one on the beach who was not topless, and I joked, saying that her modesty was out of place, since no one took any notice. Then I was to have a dream that we were on holiday in Italy, and had been to a swim pool, after which she decided to go around topless in the town, wearing only a lower bikini piece. I found there was nothing I could say about it, after having told her that no one takes any notice, although I felt she was rather overdoing things. My not knowing the language but hearing the remarks, seeing how people stared at her, and waiting in a long bus queue, then being hustled on to a bus, going down stairs where the seats were full of men, and no pair of seats available, provided enough disquiet in me to keep my mind wholly on the dream, especially when one sporty Italian, who could not keep his gaze off her, made an inviting gesture and moved swiftly over to make room for her next to himself.

In another dream I find myself friendly with an Italian family who have a café, with tables at each side. The café owner is out and the dream goes on with myself chatting to the daughter and her husband, who are tailors, and the daughter persuades me, rather against my will, to agree to order a suit. She starts measuring me, but I am able to tell her my measurements: 36-inch inside leg, 30-inch waist. (Only when I wake up and start writing down the dream do I realise that 36 is the waist and 30 the inside leg; dream facts are almost invariably wrong.) The wife of the proprietor, a plumpish woman in her forties who speaks no English, comes in and explains that she is the mother and she will measure me. The daughter interprets, then she and her husband go off serving customers, leaving me with the mother. She tells in broken English of a suit her son-in-law has made – oh, what a lovely suit, and she makes a sweep of her hand to indicate a slimmed-in waist. No, I explain, I want a plain waist, a loose-fitting jacket, but this she does not understand. I turn to her and put my hand on her stomach – and find that the loose pinafore she is wearing is open and my hand is on her warm naked skin, which is a pleasant feeling. No, I explain, not tight, but loose, and I hold my hand two inches in front of her. She shakes her head, doesn't grasp what I mean. Against what I feel is a wiser prompting, I put my hand on her stomach again, which she seems to enjoy – as do I, and although I am taking a liberty I realise we are standing in the middle of the café near the door, so my intentions are no more than flippant. Not this, I explain, pressing my hand on her naked stomach. As I do so the door opens and her husband enters. He goes into a terrible temper with her, and then when he sees it is me he can't believe it. She was only measuring me for a suit, I explain, trying not to look guilty. Measuring you! he cries, with your arms around her! What a way to measure you!

I wake up. I have left the electric heater on in my bed, and the bed has become too warm.

An impulsion in most dreaming, which works fluently because it re-echoes a similar sensation in daily life, is the Compliance of Obedience Factor. We are used to complying to the social pattern expected from us, and although we might breakfast in pyjamas and dressing gown, we make sure we don't go to work dressed in that manner. If we drive off in a car to work in the morning we keep to the left or right as told, we usually stop where it says Stop, and if a notice tells us that our usual route is closed, we take the alternative directed route. If we travel by bus or train we must at once make that inner switch of feeling by which we resign ourselves to being controlled by some unseen power with which we have no contact, let alone control over. It is as though we feel some omnipotent authority to be over us, the way we intuitively submit to signs, orders and to those individuals wearing uniforms. (Certain spirited or ego-istic children resist, but almost all finally give in – if not they usually end up in prison or in some other institution.) Dream-ing is made simpler by the fact of our being conditioned, regi-mented, so to speak, which means we tend not to think outside the dream situation – never question, never object, and allow ourselves to be pushed along by events. Linked to compliance are expectancy and novelty factors.

The first day I got my bank card, with its secret pin code, I went into town, saw a metal cash machine attached to the wall outside a bank, went up to it, looked at the people passing by to make sure I wasn't being watched too closely, took out my card, read the order, 'Insert Card', made to put it in, but the card would not go in, then I realised I was holding it the wrong side up, so I turned it round, and the card disappeared down the slot. On a small screen came the message 'Please wait'. I waited, then came the message "Enter personal number', and I pressed the four digits – 5055. There followed a series of queries and instructions. How much money did I want, and did I need any other transaction. Obediently I did everything I was ordered to, there was a final clicking and waiting, then out came nine £10 and two £5 notes. The next customer, a plump woman, smiled at me, and I said, 'I've backed a winner again…' and she said, 'Good lad you!' I stood there in the street with the £100 in my hand, and I was aware of the Novelty Factor, the experience having been like a brief dream – a not unpleasant one, reminding me of when I was a boy and enjoyed putting a coin into a machine and a bar of chocolate coming out.

Another aspect of this experience, as in dreams, might be called the Disappointing Factor. The next time I went there, in full confidence to draw my hundred pounds, I inserted my card, gave my number on the digits, dilly-dallied a bit, peered in at the lights which suddenly began to flash in and out, and the next thing the thick plastic frame came down over the machine and shut me off. I was left standing in the street with no bank card and no money. I went into the bank to enquire. 'It must've captured your card,' said the clerk, 'it does if you don't operate it within so many seconds. Sorry, but it won't be opened now until tomorrow morning.' So I went off with empty pockets, feeling the way I feel in a dream when things go against me.

An idea, a new and novel one, will excite and engage me almost as much as an emotion in dreams – but may not grip me as tight. Such dreams invariably come to me at early morning, after I have been awake and up for two or three hours, had tea and toast and usually done some writing (there is no better time for it), which means my mind is active in the ideas area. Of many such dreams here are two associated with the *New Yorker* magazine, which was often my main form of light reading. I had the following dream one morning during a half-hour sleep (between seven a.m. and seven thirty a.m.).

I dreamt that it is a bright morning, the scene a large Victorian room, with typists and a clerk or two around, my wife and myself, and I am about to begin work on a novel. Before starting, however, I see a copy of the *New Yorker* and decide to open it. Inside is a series of detailed and impressive cartoons, each covering two pages, and produced in such as way that no one has to turn the magazine sideways to see the drawings at full length. 'I often can't make out what these jokes are about,' I say to a man who is standing beside me. 'Look at this one,' I go on, 'just look!' This man and myself look at the cartoon, on which there are a number of people, down the middle are three desks, with a typist at each. 'From the look,' I say, 'I'd say this was supposed to be around 1910.' The machines have curious little cubes on them, and I wonder if it is some hint of a new silicon chip of today and vaguely feel it might have to do with coal-filling days (for this is the way coal is now often transformed in my dreams). Each typist on the drawing is set ready to work on her machine, and there are a number of men standing around, wearing old-fashioned clothes. There is a man in a morning suit at the centre of the proceedings, but placed down at the bottom on the left hand side of the cartoon. He has a hand raised and is just calling out: 'Right, everybody – let's start on Chapter Five!' I turn to the man beside me and say, 'I can't believe they have made such a big drawing for such a little joke.' Then as I think about it and start admiring the detail, I find I am thinking it funny – a big scene, everybody ready to start on a chapter in a book. The thought also strikes me that it's not a bad little idea at that, for I often feel I could do with some help of that sort to set me going on my almost finished book.

'Funny thing,' I say to the man, 'but for a time when I was in London writing film scripts that was exactly what I had – three typists I could dictate to.' (They could only come for a couple of hours in the morning, and often I had three together.) Then I decide I must show my wife this particular joke. Some dream hunch warns me against doing so but I override this warning and go to her. Then I discover I can find every cartoon except this one. The magazine is full of them, each one detailed and well drawn, and I look at them closely, but I cannot find the one I have been seeking. When I woke up and thought it over I wondered at the ingenuity of the Dream Mind, that it could instantly produce a magazine full of detailed drawings.

*Dream*: I open a copy of the *New Yorker* magazine and my interest is at once caught by an *animated* cartoon in which the characters actually move around on the page and speak out. How clever of them, I think as I hear the voices, to conjure up an idea like that! On the cartoon I see two men carrying a sedan chair, which strikes me at once as a comic sight, looking like a small wheel-less coach, the contraption supported on long poles, one man in front and one behind. They stop at what could be the front of a stage in a theatre, and from the side of the sedan a man with the rubbery face of a comedian looks out and calls, 'My wife is from Bel Air...' then he adds, '... fuck her!' Next time he gets out, pauses, and corrects himself, 'No ... Bel Tuckit ... fuck it!' There was no caption, and I thought, that's most extraordinary, the *New Yorker* is now doing talking cartoons, but they can't be charged with pornography because nothing is written down.

Associations: the evening before my wife and I had talked over various ways of how one of our cats could be got into a cat basket to be taken to the vet, and we had toyed about with different covered baskets. Also, I had remarked to her on a change to the more free and sexy stories in the *New Yorker*. Before going to bed I had pointed out a book advert in which the Booker Prize was displayed, the B being crossed out and an F substituted. I had heard something on the radio to the effect that in law pornography refers entirely to printed words and does not include spoken words.

I had a long dream of which the final scene was as follows. A mother has introduced her small son to me, aged about five, flaxen-haired and blue-eyed, a child with a most innocent expression, and I chat to him warmly, make jokes, and he laughs and chats back. Then suddenly he says to me, 'Oh you are lovely!' 'Me – lovely!' I laugh out loud. 'But I'm an old man,' I tell him, 'and old men are not lovely!' The boy turns his serious gaze on me, and says in a quiet voice, 'I can't see – I'm blind – and to me all people are lovely.' I woke up at that moment and found I had tears in my eyes.

# 18

## *Moral Pointers in Dreams*

I shall repeat that the factors influencing our dreams are so subtle, covert, diverse and multifold, that any determination of them we usually light upon by chance of waking up. (There is a sound reason why the immediate post-sleep period, despite its lethargy, if tapped, should prove fecund in ideas and insights.) A seemingly forgotten memory of a childhood bully, a spasm of jealousy from youth, or a wisp of guilt will propel an old man's dreams. As Freud points out: 'A humiliation that was experienced thirty years ago acts exactly like a fresh one throughout thirty years.' (The freshness, I suggest, is the consequence of a dream regression, one in which the requisite neurons are activated, and the dreamer becomes more the self of the earlier period.) In old age an adolescent sexual desire can be smuggled into dreams as easily as something seen or spoken of before going to bed. (These intuitive nudges the dreamer alone can sense – usually with the dream warm in mind.) All's grist that comes to the mill of the Dream Mind – from a whim to a close secret.

A conscientious scruple will motivate a series of dreams

as surely as any sense of guilt – of which the following is an example. In my youth I had a good pal called Jack, of whom I was fond, but we had lost touch for many years; then after my having had some success in the theatre, I used often think how I should enjoy the opportunity of repaying Jack his many kindnesses to me in the old days. With that thought on my mind, Jack kept turning up in my dreams, which pleased me, except that he was always in company, and that meant we could never have a good chat together. During these many dreams I go around with a useful sum in my pocket to slip to Jack, but either he fails to turn up, or he does so with others, and I never make good my wish. Thinking over these dreams during the day, and recalling our happy times together, prompted me to make more determined enquiries about my old pal, and I sent letters to the town in which he had been active in politics. I got no reply, and decided that either Jack must be dead or didn't want to see me. Later I had the following dream about him. I dreamt that Jack turned up alone for an early breakfast one morning. It delighted me to see him so well, wearing an astrakhan hat (he was a Marxist and had always taken a lively interest in Russia). I felt sure this was going to be the chance for a good talk, and my learning how things were with him, perhaps being able to help him in some way, but Jack told me that he had brought a few trade-union friends along, and that they were waiting outside. This news disappointed me keenly, but I hid my feelings, and told him to bring them all in. There were five, and they chatted over politics at the table – not my favourite subject – whilst I cooked bacon and eggs for them;

and after much trouble some bubble-and-squeak, as an extra treat (leftover bacon, cabbage and potatoes from the previous evening). This cooking kept me occupied during most of the dream whilst Jack and his mates were eating, so I got no chance of the few words I had hoped to have with him. Jack's friends excluded me from their chat, as though I were some lackey, and I felt disillusioned, let down and rather sad about the whole thing. They all went off without a word of thanks, and when I went to pick up their plates, I saw that each one had noticeably left his bubble-and-squeak, pushed it aside on the plate, as though such a homely dish was not even worth their attention. That really annoyed me and I thought, to hell with the lot of them – I'm not going out of my way to please anybody. Since that dream I haven't dreamt of Jack at all, and have a feeling I've finished with those dreams – or these dreams with me. (My thwarted attempts to meet Jack alone may simply have been a dream device to keep up the pursuit and ensure more dreams.)

Any person brought up in working class life – such as myself, who eased out of it in my thirties – and has since acquired particular skills, those of a writer for instance, cannot but feel some prick of conscience at the sums he can often earn for a piece of writing, compared with the pittance paid to the heavy worker for a week's strenuous labour. I rarely felt it over a dozen early years of a writing life, when I could just make ends meet, but after I became successful I often had a twinge, but had to keep the feeling to myself – which secrecy helps to ferment a potent dream brew, of which the following is an example.

*Dream*: A lunch has taken place at the Garrick Club to set up a film deal, and agreement has been reached, with myself engaged to write the script. The atmosphere has been most cordial, with much high flown talk over the food, wine, coffee, brandy and cigars, each one present coming up with his own little idea; the producer, the agent, lawyers and others have all chipped in about how the script should be written. I have largely agreed with everyone – knowing from experience it is the wisest course, since argument is not only futile but draining of energy – yet at the same time have been uneasily aware that the ideas which sound so good over a festive table will have a way of not working out when I get home and down to the actual writing. Only when one is alone and working will the snags reveal themselves, I tell myself, with some foreboding. As I am preparing to leave the restaurant, together with the film and city people, enjoying the sense of luxury and privilege with my new and famous acquaintances, a right matey lot the are, with the waiters looking on and smiling with a sort of strained good humour, I realise I have been made not unaware of a sense of my own importance as a writer – for they have all been more or less addressing their remarks to me, and handing over ideas for me to work out – and now in a slightly boozed daze I go alone to the rack in the cloakroom on which the coats are hung. It seems to be empty, and I look for the dark expensive overcoat which I have left there, but cannot see it. Then to my astonishment I discover in its place in the corner is a splendid coal-bagger's coat.

I take it up in my hands, a big double-breasted jacket, woolly, warm and comfortably substantial, the front of rich grey corduroy, with huge flap pockets, the back of thick moleskin, which could turn a day's rain, the whole thing snugly lined with heavy wool material. I even put it to my face, this most distinctive garment, for it brings back so many memories, and then I put it on, there in the cloakroom of the West End restaurant. The moment is filled with a sort of near enchantment, and in the dream I have a most nostalgic memory of the day when I was issued with my first new coal-bagger's jacket, which I tried on in the cookhouse of Lark Street stables in Bolton on a wet cold winter evening in 1936. I recall the excitement of getting into it, and of how that coat seemed to fit so perfectly that I was hardly aware of having it on, except for that gush of warmth that at once pervaded my body. 'I'll go home in it,' I had said, as I put it over my thin jacket.

Standing there in the Garrick Club, flushed with old memories, my heart sinks as I realise that this splendid garment is no longer of any use to me, for now I cannot wear it. Then I turn to survey myself in the big mirror, and warm to the sight and feel of the big corduroy jacket, but as my gaze moves upward I see a face that could be that of a stranger, puffy and suffused from food and wine, and something prompts me to ask myself: *Have I gone up in the world – as everybody seems to imagine – or have I come down?* I woke up. Then lying there in the darkness, and recalling the old days, and all my working mates, I knew the answer to that question.

Drama and excitement, blended with danger, will create vivid dreaming, but anticipation also has a good pull. In dreams with an anticipatory incentive, however, there is the risk that the plum or the carrot dangled before the dreamer is likely to be from some longing of the past, one which no longer exercises the same attraction. This will not impede the dream flow at the start, since the Dream Mind will have evoked the dream self at one with the period of the dream – the child, the boy or the youth. What happens as the dream proceeds, however, is that there is an intrusion of awareness – caused by some glancing thought which breaks in, mixing a flicker of contemporary reality with the dream happenings. The dream continues – it must, since themes cannot be changed – but the hold on the dreamer has weakened. My own way of life, having been transformed from that of a manual worker to that of a writer, the contrast between the past and the present is an exceptional one. Although the change occurred forty years ago the Dream Mind often fails to take this into account, simply because some of the most deep-seated experiences of my life took place during that earlier period when I was hard up. To me the interesting aspect of such dreams is how swiftly the Dream Mind makes a cunning ploy which recoups the loss of drama and regains full control over me – and my present self. The following is an example:

*Dream:* I feel very much myself, but am a young man back on my old coal-bagging job, seated beside the carter on a pile of sacks making our way on the horse-drawn lorry through the narrow streets of Bolton to the coal siding. (This particular vein of feeling is keenly struck in the dream, for it occurred daily over the impressionable years of my early twenties.) The mood is propitious, the day being the Saturday which starts the annual holiday week, so that in addition to the weekend off there is also the prospect of a full week's rest. (How should I know that it is since, so far as I am aware, I haven't been told? This is intimated by what I call the Dream Sprite, without the dreamer being aware of the fact.)

Added to the excitement is the thought that on this morning every year, the usual weighman for checking the weight of the load will not be on duty, and in his place will be a yardman who can neither count nor reckon up; nor will there be any of the firm's inspectors about, for they are all away, too, and so with a bit of luck it is going to be a simple matter for the carter to put an extra bag or two of coal on the lorry, so as to make a few shillings on the side for him and myself to share. These impressions harmonise in the dream, so that on this Saturday morning it is bliss to be alive, and heaven to be a coal-bagger. Even old mare Dinah has caught the festal mood, for clopping across Waterloo Street, breaking wind with every step, she moves like a filly.

Suddenly there sneaks in a glimpse of my present self: Don't forget that though you might be coal-bagging, it whispers, you are a writer, so why are you getting so excited over a few shillings and a week's holiday? My dream self of some fifty years earlier, an eager and spirited young man in his twenties, with a wife and two children, glad of any extra money that might come his way, now feels that some of the fun and purpose has been taken out of life, and sitting there on the pile of sacks becomes dispirited. To compensate for this I take up a detached attitude, see myself as a man above temptation, and resolve to forgo any bunce we might get, and let the carter have the lot. A writer lives by honesty, I start telling myself, and must allow nothing to pollute his conscience. We drive in through the wide open gates of siding, the carter looks around and draws down a narrow run and halts the horse-and-lorry beside a likely wagon of coal: 'I think we'll ha' this'n, Billy,' he says to me. I nod in agreement, and can't help but think that with no one about what an ideal spot it would make for slipping in an extra bag or two.

Despite the setback, it is a warmly familiar moment as I pick up the big coal shovel, duck down under the low door, and stand inside the wagon ready for work. I look around but am puzzled at the sight – there is not a nut of coal in sight! That's odd, I think to myself; but then I see that the wagon is not empty but loaded in the corners with what appear to be dark amber bricks of one kind or another. Funny kind of coal, I think, and am mystified for the moment. I take up one of the bricks in my hand and am astonished at the weight of it. I scratch the surface with my thumbnail and suddenly realise what it is – *a gold ingot!*

Well fancy that, gold ingots piled up all around the coal wagon! There are hundreds of them, thousands in fact – and from the casual way they've been flung one on top of the other, it is clear they haven't been counted or checked. My heart gives a funny twist at the sight of all that gold. Not that I am personally interested in gold, I tell myself, but just think what some people would give to be in my shoes – Bolton Holiday Saturday, no weighman about, and all this gold lying around in a coal wagon! And these ingots are such a nice handy size, solid but not bulky – one or two would fit nicely into the big pockets of my corduroy working jacket without being noticed. Indeed they might have been made for that very purpose.

Of course this does put a different complexion on things. I mean with the price of gold these days each one must be worth at least ten thousand pounds, or possibly twenty or more. It seems true that there is this special thrill about handling solid gold – I can even feel it in my fingers. Gold, they say, never loses its value. And who in this world can it harm if a few of these go missing! In fact they wouldn't be missed. True enough, I am a writer, and certainly not interested in money as such, yet it must be admitted that a few gold ingots tucked away on one side despite my being a successful writer, might come in very handy in an emergency. Yes, very handy indeed – and I pick one up.

I awoke, and it seemed that my hands were sweating a bit from handling that gold ingot. Then lying there in the dark I went over the dream, savouring every moment of it, but most of all those last ones. I had to marvel at the cunning of the Dream Mind, how when reason sneaked in, it was soon matched and hoodwinked; then how easily it enticed me, by transforming coal into gold, laying bare any illusion I might harbour about my own ethical standards. It seemed that various inferences of character could be gleaned from such a dream, but as it was such a searching interpretation of me, the notion of my telling it to an analyst, and he or she attempting to interpret or analyse it, would seem ludicrous to me.

# 19

## *Writing and Dreaming*

'I've never sat down and said to myself – "Now, I'm going to write a poem!"' wrote James Stephens, the Irish poet. 'It really happened the other way about, and I had very little to say in the matter.' What is spoken of as the 'imagination' or 'creativity' affirms the flair of certain persons to receive intimations from the Superconscious – the artist having the aptitude, skills and volition to express them. My practice of starting writing almost on waking up, made me more aware than are most people of this imaginational agency that operates in dreaming; vestiges of it can often be felt during the immediate post-sleep period, when problems that baffled one are unexpectedly solved, and the writing flows without hesitancy or much thought, asking for no more than a certain form of concentration. Once those billions of cells become excited, that is the time to be writing; never say, 'I'll remember that and write it down later,' the active synapses must be caught on the move or the freshness is lost. Trollope is known for having done almost all his writing before breakfast, timing himself to progress at a rate of 250 words every quarter of an hour.

Writing fiction seems to me to be the positive form of conscious dreaming, providing packaged dreams for others, and once the aspirant has mastered the art, fiction provides an imaginary re-living of the writer's life – one in some instances as different from the actual circumstances as dreaming is from daily life – in a medium in which others may share; a certain pertinacity in getting the work done will often provide a lucrative living, or at least a satisfying one. Writing, like reading, may become something of an addiction. Although in the early years it may prove a difficult undertaking, yet once one has acquired some feeling of the craft, seen the emerging of characters, the narrative and plot taking shape, few occupations can prove so rewarding, as the sentence takes on a rhythm and the whole thing begins to flow. Good fiction, like dreaming, demands an emotive pulse to keep it going, but this needs to be kept under control – a flood of emotion being no use in either medium.

Regarding avid readers who cannot bear to be separated from a novel until they have imbibed it, and then, as after a dream, forget all about it, I gather that there are writers who can do the same. They are skilled at some form of hack work, crime or romance novels, and apparently sit down at around nine every morning and more or less write anything that comes into mind for two or three hours – doubt or hesitation is fatal, as in a dream flow – then they get up and put it out of mind until they sit down next morning, get the Dream Mind in gear, and away they go. 'I wrote 1,100 words of *Under the Hammer* in one and a half hours. Great going,' wrote Arnold Bennett in his diary. 'Considering I only slept two hours last night I was in astonishing creative form.' That, I would suggest, was why he was in such good form, because he had slept and dreamt for such a short time, and was enjoying the surplus energy that would have been spent on dreaming. (Not, I must point out, that I consider Arnold Bennett was a hack, far from it, although he prided himself on never refusing an acceptable commission; he was outstanding in everything to which he turned his brilliant mind, but his best writing in my opinion is in his journals, for he was a superb diarist. Incidentally, writers are usually able to record more vivid and interesting dreams than non-writers.)

Joyce's *Ulysses* is a peculiar exercise in imaginative autobiography, in which certain memories, sensitively private to the author – including humbled pride, prurience, and various forms of jealousy, together with a need for a sort of revenge – are given expression in a story, all cunningly encapsulated in a single day in Dublin. Edmund Wilson noted that James Joyce wrote the sort of speech that emerges in dreams, but no one seems to have pointed out that many patches of prose in Joyce are what could be called *dream prose*. By that I mean that he cultivated a technique by which he nudged himself into a sort of dreamlike state to start writing. According to his sister Eileen, Joyce wrote mostly at night, lying on his stomach across the bed, wearing a white coat. Joyce's main characters, such as Leopold Bloom and Stephen Dedalus, are of a somnambulistic order, mostly wandering around alone, almost as if half-asleep. Joyce, like most writers, was intensely interested in dreams. He wrote a verse play in his youth called *Dream Stuff*; he had terrifying dreams and nightmares, was eager to hear the dreams of his friends, and made a stab at interpreting them.

*The Portrait*, almost at the opening, employs a dreamlike memory of a child wetting his bed; *Ulysses* ends with Molly Bloom in bed, indulging a prolonged near-hypnagogic monologue; *Finnegans Wake* is a night book and something of a dream from start to finish, and no prose or poem of Joyce's is without some dreamlike passage. What is perhaps his most quoted passage at the end of the short story, 'The Dead', is intense with those murmurings that creep in before going to sleep: 'He watched sleepily the flakes, silver and dark … falling softly … softly falling … His soul swooned slowly as he heard the snow falling faintly … and faintly falling.' I believe it is this almost subliminal approach of Joyce that allowed the epiphanies to emerge and so richly illuminate his writing. It may well be that the true fascination Joyce has for his devoted readers is that he is a unique artificer of dream prose, and he creates this tight evocative mood which has an almost hypnotic effect upon those who are susceptible to it, and which leaves cold those who are not. In *The Waste Land* T.S. Eliot strings together a variety of seemingly unrelated thoughts, fancies and feelings with such skilful dreamlike diction, of a hypnotising rhythm and flow, that undermines critical attention – although it would seem that Ezra Pound achieved a considerable improvement when he persuaded the poet to cut the original down by half.

I am merely sketching in the intrinsic weft of the dream present in all literature, one given insufficient attention by critics – and for each writer I mention a reader will be able to recall a dozen of his own. Proust, with his cork-lined bedroom and habit of writing in bed, is an obvious example of a superb dream-fed writer. An equally brilliant artificer of a dream-inspired writer was Franz Kafka. He had little or no interest in being published, understandable in one who is his own judge, and writes from some inner compulsion (his 'dream-like inner life'), and is largely indifferent to public praise or disparagement. Kafka came to mind as I was writing down a dream of wandering alone inside a vast refrigerating plant. Ice was being manufactured somewhere in the background, but the area I moved about in had numerous groups of workers, who were idling and didn't know quite how to pass their time. I wanted to get out of the place, and I asked different men for the way out, and although friendly they were vague in their replies; no one actually refused to tell me, but each one dodged giving a definitive reply. Finally, after much anxiety and frustration, I started crying, and just opened my heart to them all, as it were, and although they were obviously moved by my plight, they did nothing to help me get out. Then I found myself sitting in a sort of train, still in the place, and as more men got in I found I couldn't breathe. I cried out and woke up.

And even if we elevate ourselves almost out of this world to that of Shakespeare – also allowing that there were other versions of such plays long before he wrote his own – we may ask how much unlike a dream is *Hamlet* or *Macbeth*? There is the ghost, the murder and incest themes, the uncertainties and dreamlike indecision, the misunderstandings and the ending with all the main characters dead – almost any or all of this could be dreamt. The play within a play, a device also used in *A Midsummer Night's Dream*, I take to reflect the 'dream within a dream'. In *Macbeth* we have the witches upon the heath, the prophecy that Macbeth shall be king, the murder of Duncan, the witches again, the murder of Banquo, the haunting by the ghost, the murder of Lady Macbeth and her children, even to Birnan Wood apparently coming to Dunsinane. The rich and striking imagery of Shakespeare, the unique felicity of language, are testimony to the power of the Dream Mind; his ramshackle plots – which any theatre hack could have improved – he wisely ignored, knowing that what would work was the drama and poetry. As Dr Johnson remarked of him: 'He had no regard to distinction of time or place, but gives to one age or nation, without scruple, the customs, institutions and opinions of another, at the expense not only of likelihood, but of possibility.' It is exactly so, of course, in the dream.

There are certain books, such as *Don Quixote, Alice's Adventures in Wonderland*, to which I could add *Huckleberry Finn, Moby Dick, King Arthur and the Knights of the Round Table*, and almost all the fairy tale stories of Hans Andersen, which not only achieved enormous popularity – sometimes of an esoteric nature – but do not suffer much from change of fashion, and draw new readers from varied generations, often over centuries, when other books, possibly superior from a literary aspect, are long forgotten. My own belief is that each of these is created on a Dream Mind flow – which is unchanging. If this same substratum takes hold of the reader – it fails to in many cases – a passionate disciple is made, and it is passion, not mere liking, which creates the response needed to make a classic. Such books appear to have in common what would in other books appear to be a failing, and that is that they almost never quite come to the point, or if they do it is not the point the reader has been led to expect – another similarity to the dream.

One reason why long hours of sleep are not good for a writer – or for anyone engaged in 'creative' work – is that prolonged dreaming impoverishes the imaginative flow, the reserve essential to writing. 'Our mind is so fortunately equipped, that it brings us the most important bases for our thoughts without our having the least knowledge of this work of elaboration,' wrote Wundt. 'Only the results of it become conscious. This unconscious mind is for us like an unknown being who creates and produces for us, and finally throws the ripe fruits in our lap.'

## 20

# *Films, Plays and Opera*

The success of the first motion pictures in the early part of the century was phenomenal. I remember sitting with a bunch of mates, huddled together on the hard wooden benches comprising the front rows of the Derby Picture Palace in 1922, the atmosphere fuggy, smelling of sweaty cotton-mill workers and orange peel. The excitement as the safety curtain began to roll up was unbearable, and cheers and cries broke out, then silence as the lights were lowered, and the little white dot from the projection box began to dance around the centre of the white screen, and finally the thrill as the hush fell upon the audience and the pictures began. It was not entertainment but sheer enchantment.

The utter fascination of movies, I am convinced, was and is in their being a vicarious form of dreaming. The basic similarity between dreaming and watching a movie is of course the immediacy of both experiences, and the sense of involvement. As for the converse – the dream copying the film, I have had numerous dreams which purport to be films I am watching. This comes about, I suppose, because the imaginative fertility demanded for fresh dreams is lacking, and what must serve is a form of second-class dreaming – it engages as entertainment, but the grip is not as keen. Sometimes I get an inkling of the film being a memory rerun of one I have seen years earlier, although some dreams are originals, and as scene after scene goes on, with cuts, mixes and dissolves, I find I am thinking to myself: Can this only be a dream I am dreaming – it seems impossible that all these ideas and images can be produced at such speed from nothing, or am I actually in a cinema watching? The following is what on awakening I felt sure was a repeat of one I had seen.

*Dream*: I am watching a black-and-white movie, sitting fairly close to the screen, so that it is all exceptionally vivid. The scene is a shop of a sinister kind, a front for some racket in drugs and crime, with various counters and shelves of glossy timber, and a man in charge who has a far-east Asian look. We cut from the shop to meet a cheery young reporter who is being sent to investigate the set-up. He is wearing a double-breasted overcoat which is unfastened, a trilby hat, and he has an easygoing and unsuspecting manner. He doesn't know where the shop is, but he has the address on a piece of paper, and he stops to ask a shopkeeper, another far-east Asian, who is standing outside his shop, how should he get there. The man looks at the address on the paper, and explains to the reporter the way to get there, waves him off all smiling; then his expression changes as he hurries into his shop, and is seen talking into an old-fashioned telephone. Voices are not heard, but sounds are – and we take it that he is warning the man in the first shop. We go back to the reporter, a real innocent he is, the carefree manner in which he strolls along; then stops and stands outside the shop, and all unsuspecting goes inside. We go in with him, and detect an ominous atmosphere of emptiness about it, of which the young reporter seems unaware as he goes around inspecting things in a casual fashion. Suddenly a door partly opens, a hand appears and grabs the reporter by the back of the collar of his overcoat, and jerks him out of sight. That shot was fumbled a bit, I think to myself, not clean or crisp enough. Now all is quiet in the shop as I gaze at the closed door. The next moment the door opens and a large tray is pushed out along the floor, as the door shuts. On the tray, all neatly piled, are the reporter's clothes, shirt, tie, socks, shoes, overcoat, and on top the trilby hat. I feel a little quake of fear, and think, my goodness, they've soon got rid of him!

Now the scenes follow swiftly, with another reporter coming to investigate what has happened to his colleague (Richard Widmark playing the part in the dream). But he is no innocent, for before entering the shop he pauses, opens his double-breasted raincoat, and fingers the blade of a long-handled axe, which is concealed down the left-hand side of his coat. From his grim look he is clearly the sort of man who will use it should there be trouble. He inspects the empty shop, hands in pockets, sees a door open and enters. At once there is a flurry of activity in the shop, with new wooden fixtures being slid into place all round, transforming the place, and shutting off all on the other side. The effect is claustrophobic. What has happened to our hero with the axe? Nothing happens for moments, then a strange sound is heard. At first it is impossible to say where it is coming from, but the next thing the new fittings are shaking. The blade of the axe is seen cleaving an opening in the timbered shop fitments. In moments Richard Widmark has cut an opening big enough to allow himself to step out from behind it all, and stand there, axe in hand, ready for all contingencies. (I will not continue the film, which was a long one, but when I was writing it down and recalling it with utter clarity, I thought of the scriptwriters who would have sweated for days over the scenes that were running before me, unbidden out of some corner of my memory. I am now rather sorry I didn't record all of it.)

The elusive influence of the Dream Mind can be detected, but never quite pinned down, in every medium of the arts, but possibly in none so much as that of drama. Although the unpredictable presence, which differentiates craft from intuition in the theatre, does not allow of it being spoken of except in such terms as 'stardust', yet the good actors and directors are aware of there being *something*. They know it is not all talent and experience, since these can be brought into service and the venture fail. The wide respect paid to superstition in the theatre, which is never wholly ignored, may indicate this sense of the supernormal.

To watch the early rehearsals of a play it is as though a group of people had got together to create or concoct (according to motivation, whether it be artistic or mercenary) a dream for an audience. First there is the writer, who has 'dreamt up' the idea, and written it in the form he feels will most engage an audience, then the director, who thinks up the likely actors to portray the characters, and decides on all the moves, next the designer – and later the lighting man to make it all more dreamlike; there is of course the cast, each one of which is perhaps less interested in the total play than in his or her particular part, but whose combined efforts will decide whether or not the dream is successful. I have seen an actress playing a key role, but one it seems she either doesn't understand or prefers not to. She is not concerned about the play, only her own lines, which she marks boldly on her script. She often forgets or changes them, messes up rehearsals, argues with the director, makes everyone apprehensive. Then comes the opening night, she goes on the stage and almost at once electrifies the audience. The playwright is only too glad to accept the character alive on the stage and forget the character he first envisaged. With such a performer it is as though she inhabits a dream mood every time she appears on stage: and when the play has finished its run the lines in which she was word perfect will be forgotten in a day, as in a dream.

For a play to succeed there needs to be implanted in it or at least touching on it in some way, a sense of myth (the myth being the creation of the Primal Intelligence, from which the Dream Mind functions). That is why plays about kings and queens, murderers and maniacs will often succeed, whereas a good play about industrial working folk will not. These classes have not yet created sufficient myth about themselves, apart from strikes and the hunger marchers, for few myths can be created among machinery in factories. Peasants have their myths – as we have seen in the plays of Synge – and so have seamen and rural labourers, but the engineer has little myth to him. As the lights dim in the theatre and the curtain rises, one can feel the mood of the audience, sense an appetite for some novel scene, something to enchant if possible, or to amuse and entertain, but certainly to engage, so that they can shed all self-awareness for an hour or two, and give themselves up to the play. The designer should be able to evoke a gasp of surprise or delight as the curtain rises, and the playwright should strive not to let the audience down on their first sight of the stage. Chekhov had this instinct about what would work in the theatre, down to the very titles: *The Cherry Orchard*, *The Three Sisters*, each one a sort of romantic image, which already touches an audience. He also knew the need for a certain guiding indirectness: any speech that is 'on the nose' – too blunt or literal, does not work well, it is better to hint than state. A line in Brecht's play *Galileo* makes a frightening impact, 'Don't torture him – just let him see the instruments.' This sort of thing leaves it to the imagination – the same is mostly so in dreams.

In a dream every happening must make its impact instantly and produce the calculated reaction. A skilfully written play would develop in the same way, employing such inherent progression as a technique. A start of some kind is needed, of course: expecting a visitor, going on a journey, snowbound in a hotel, stuck down the mine, searching for someone, a murder has been committed or, as often happens in a dream, just waiting. A theatre audience should be held lightly or tightly by the dream and situation – the grip eased to allow temporary relaxation by injections of comedy (too much laughter and you lose them, unrelieved drama and you exhaust them), but what no theatre audience should be expected to do is *think*.

Thought neutralises drama; in the theatre as in dreaming. The intellect, as the Greeks knew, has its home in the academy and not the theatre. Drama serves a perhaps more important function than to educate, which is to inspire. The audience reacting solely to what it hears and sees, as in the dream, should be kept in a state approaching *conscious dreaming*. (Anyone looking for education in dreams would gather a hotchpotch of misinformation.) A woman onstage, about whom we are told of the loss of her uninsured home and the deaths of her nine children in a fire will compel our theatre sympathy less keenly than a man who is actually seen chopping firewood and gets a tiny splinter in his finger, then hops around in pain before our eyes. Retrospective drama has to be told, and this demands thought, and thinking runs counter to the imagination. (In almost no other medium are the class and culture divisions obliterated or non-existent as in the theatre and cinema with the gallery audience as vital as that of the dress circle.)

Acting mimics conscious dreaming, with the actor going out of his present self to become for a time an assumed self. I have found that an actor will always choose a somewhat unreal role, such as Hamlet, to that of a solid and understandable character; good actors give of their best to Beckett, Pinter and Genet. Ionesco who has had two plays, *The Bald Soprano* and *The Lesson* running for twenty-five years at a Paris theatre, told in an interview how he works: 'I work in the morning. I sit comfortably in an armchair opposite my secretary; luckily, although she's intelligent, she knows nothing about literature … I speak slowly, and she takes it down. I let characters and symbols emerge from me, as if I were dreaming. I always use what remains of my dreams of the night before. Dreams are reality at its most profound, and what you invent is truth because invention, by its nature, can't be a lie.' (Imagine the potential loss of material to any playwright who is unfamiliar with his dream life!)

Corresponding to this, the audience in a theatre gives itself up most happily to what is in effect a *dream* set. Should the scene be a poor home, a prison cell or a public urinal there must be smuggled into it by deft colour and lighting a touch of charm. A play that does not attract – even repulsively – will not hold an audience. Nobody looks for a realistic set, since the audience do not, but the fact that they are an audience means they are willing to suspend disbelief – at least for an hour or two. And as in a dream they should be made believe in the utter reality of it all: a word that must never arise in the mind of an audience or a dreamer is, *Why?*

As to music in a play I will give a simple example of what happened in a play of my own, set in a working-class home, which in one scene the company gather round the piano and sing by firelight. It was decided that in case the actress who played the piano was off sick, there should be a tape, over which they could also sing. The recording date was arranged, but when they got to the studio it was found that the only piano available was a magnificent concert piano. Nothing could be done about it, so it was taped, the pianist accompanying the song on this splendid piano. Because of the contrast in tone between the pianos it was accepted that the tape could never be used, but one evening the pianist was off, and with some trepidation the tape was used. The effect was magical, quite beyond anything produced by the fidelity of playing the actual piano on the stage. After that the recording was always used, the audience loved the scene – and no one, so far as I was aware, ever questioned the producing of such tones from an old upright piano. Drama is like a dream in that the audience are in a state similar to that of the imagination during sleep – they are not watchful and circumspect, but keyed up and ready to join in any exciting and emotional scene.

Among various theatre dreams I have had was the following: I am in the shoe department of a large store, a number of supervisors going about but no one serving customers. There comes into the scene two friends of mine who are about to have a play put on at the store. A porter starts explaining how a play must be presented under the store's method of production; he sweeps the curtain back and we are standing up beside a bed on top of which an old-fashioned love scene is being played, reminiscent of a much earlier period. There is something in this method, I tell myself but my friends and everyone else disappear, and after some time, when I go into the theatre, I am the only person there in the auditorium, apart from a young man in the front row, with a notebook, a drama critic. Onstage there is a huge company, seemingly in an unhappy mess over the final rehearsal. The producer, who has his wife and family there, with the wife preparing a meal, explains to her that it will all be late, and then he starts giving an account of the play to me and the critic, the audience. I feel sorry for the company and the whole venture that things should be in such a mess.

'Of course,' says the producer, 'we have only an amateur company.' 'If you had the best professionals alive,' says the critic, 'this play is not for me – not for me!' As the two go on arguing, I slowly realise that what I am watching is not a messed-up final rehearsal, but a most skilful presentation of such. The critic who is loudly decrying the play is a member of the cast and a very good actor. I find myself enthusiastic about the idea, feeling sure that a play which criticises itself before an audience is likely to win them. I hurry off outside, and start telling the crowd to hurry up and get seats. My acclamation is such that they rush to get seats and the play is sold out. I waken up. If one's own imagination fuels one's dreams, as seems possible, and despite the echo of Pirandello, I feel I get good value from my own.

An omission from this chapter would be opera. The combination in opera of music, singing and drama so clearly induces a form of enchantment not too dissimilar from that of certain kinds of dreaming that the association makes itself. Mozart, we know, is simply magical, Beethoven most impressive, Verdi and others acutely stirring, but for those who come under his spell – he is far from the taste of everyone – Wagner imposes the most bewitching grip on an audience. If I hear an opera I usually dream of opera, but occasionally I am in such an elevated dream state that I am given a dream opera.

*Dream*: I dream that our house is a spacious building with a wing in which a composer is rehearsing a new opera. I go out on the veranda and there meet the various men singers and chat to them. They are enthusiastic about the composer, and tell me what an original character he is, a man who cares for nothing and no one, who lives only for his music. I imagine a tall man, of artistic manner, but by chance he comes out, a short thickset man, no style, no affectation, but a forceful speaker. He tells me that he won't stand for any lewdness or that sort of thing, nor for that matter can he stand any prudery – he insists on representing life in opera exactly as it is, and I agree with him. He invites me inside to hear the rehearsal, and we go in together. The stage setting is that of a bedroom, with the two leading singers, a man and a woman, getting ready to go to bed. The composer raises his baton for silence, the orchestra get ready, and without fuss he begins to conduct. The opening duet – which is the name of the opera – is 'I got to my Bed', and as they sing together, at the same time taking off their clothes, I am much drawn to how natural the whole performance is, romantic on the surface, but each one making edgy asides hinting at jealousy and suspicion, creating an uncertainty over whether or not they will make love. I had a feeling they would, but unfortunately I woke up just as they were embracing. The music and voices lingered in my mind, and I found myself taking up the attitude I had had during the dream – one of wonder that an opera could be based on such a nightly happening between a man and a woman. And for a time I marvelled that a dream could produce such a flow of song and music, and talk as well.

## 21

# *Lunch Dream – Lucid Dream*

Anachronism and asynchronism are implicitly one with dreaming: 'A slumbering thought, is capable of years,' wrote Byron. 'And curdles a long life into an hour.' This delving down into memory – as it would appear to us – to re-live some episode of the long past, is in itself a simple matter, and especially so in dreaming, with the entire history of each one of us neatly stacked away in the relevant neurons. Every face we have seen, every place we have known, every happiness and every misery, all there for the selecting. The time shift in making the past one with the present goes unnoticed by the dreamer – since all dreaming is of the moment.

In this chapter I shall give two contrasting examples from my own dreams: the first an unexciting dream, one in which I, the dreamer, am watching rather than involved, a dream in which little happens, an anticipation is all, except that by a final twist here is a realisation of the twofold dream function; in the second dream these same ends are achieved in a dramatic fashion. All that was necessary in each instance to set the dream moving was to evoke some early emotional

159

impression – a key feeling, as it were, with which I could fully identify, and be carried along by. The fusion of the two selves, alive with a latent nostalgia in which the old man is taken over by the youth or schoolboy, is a frequent contrivance of the Dream Mind. Both dreams, it might be said, achieve the simple unity of a short story or a scene from a play.

In the first dream the day is Friday and it is around one o'clock – the time when as a schoolboy I went for our Friday dinnertime meal of fish and chips. I am leaning on the counter of Booth's fish-and-chip shop in Bolton, aware of myself not as a schoolboy but a lorry driver – a role of more substance which for some years in my twenties I once filled – and I am chatting to another driver, a mate of mine. (The physical circumstances of my sleep were as follows: I had risen before six o'clock, intending to go back to bed for an hour after a light breakfast and my morning writing stint. Odd jobs prevented my going back, nor did I get any coffee; at noon, weary and hungry, I decided to rest before lunch, which meant that the dream happening coincided with actual time.)

The atmosphere in the fish-and-chip shop is more relaxed than usual, as Mr Booth, the proprietor, a big man who goes about his task of a fish-and-chip fryer in a most watchful manner, happens to be absent, and the frying is being done by his son Corny, which occasions jokes and laughter from myself and other customers. It's odd, I think, how when Mr Booth is frying you never hear laughter; he creates a serious atmosphere – that of a man doing an important job. Mr Booth is attentive to every detail of the task, carefully stocking the coal fire under the chip pans, swirling the chips around in the boiling fat, testing the occasional chip between forefinger and thumb, just to make sure it is done to perfection. Above all, the calm authority of the man, wearing his huge white apron, gives one the impression that no other person would be capable of doing the job. Yet here is Corny taking his place, making no fuss, and seemingly getting the job done just as well. It only goes to show, I think to myself, some people take their work and themselves too seriously, and I find I am all for the more relaxed way of going about life.

The dream continues, the last customers have been served by Mrs Booth, and with an easygoing smile Corny carries off his own plate of fish and chips for his dinner. (Which I had often seen him do after the early rush some sixty years earlier.) He waves to us from the kitchen where he is eating, and we keep up the banter. Mrs Booth asks me what I want, and I tell her fish and chips, but I make it threepennyworth of chips instead of the usual two, thus assuring myself of a generous portion. Chips and fish are always that bit tastier if allowed to cool down for a few minutes after cooking, and I get a nice anticipatory feeling in both mouth and stomach as I watch Mrs Booth pick up the chip shovel, then slide open the lid of the scuttle – the metal chamber on top of the range, from which the chips are served. I can hardly refrain from smacking my lips as I think how I'll give them a good dowsing with salt and vinegar to bring out the full flavour. (I tell it in detail because I dream in detail – every moment is alive with thought and sensation.) Suddenly I see her stop and her expression change: 'Hey, you!' she calls to Corny, '– what do you think you're about?' 'Why, what's up, Mam?' Corny answers from the kitchen. 'The damn thing is empty,' she tells him. 'Not a chip left. An' only one bit of fish.'

My feelings suffer an abrupt change. No chips ready! Would you believe it! And he is scoffing away, his mouth full. Why, it'll take at least another quarter of an hour to fry up another lot! And I had the thought in mind of nibbling one or two on my way home! Corny pipes back jokingly to his mother, 'All right, Mam, don't worry – I'll do a few more.' But it's no joking matter for me, and I feel myself flush with anger: 'Hey, what bloody game?' I call out to him. That's the trouble with his sort – they take it easy, but come some hitch and they let you down. 'You're not too big to do a simple job, are you!' 'What're you gettin' het up about all of a sudden?' he asks me. There he is, the cheeky sod, eating away, and me, after my morning's hard work, let down over dinner. 'About my bloody dinner,' I yell at him, 'that's what I'm het up about – an' I reckon I've every right to be. If you think you're too good for the job – don't bloody attempt it!' One thing I can't stand is being made wait for a meal once I've got a smell of it. It serves me right, I think, I should have been warned – never trust a job being done right where there's too much laughing and joking going on. But what am I to do? Do I stamp off in a temper – go hungry and keep my pride – or do I try to hold down my temper, swallow my pride, wait, and make sure of my dinner?

At that moment I am aroused by the sound of my own voice telling Corny to get a bloody move on. I wake up to find that I have slept for an hour – and what joy there is in healthy sleep! The dream had cleverly assuaged my hunger for an hour whilst I slept, and I felt very much revived, and knew just what I wanted for my next meal.

The second dream occurred when I was recovering from an attack of bronchitis, and the euphoric feeling of being able to breathe freely may have evoked the boyhood memory.

*Dream*: I am crossing the railway bridge in Rothwell Street, Bolton, on my way to school, accompanied by my sister May, she walking behind me. (The bridge was one I used only for some months, when I was thirteen years old, during an emergency after our own school had been partly destroyed by fire. The self of the dream was the self I take to be myself, neither young nor old, but in good health; I had a feeling of my sister May being my wife. The dream had merged a few keen boyhood impressions with an adult one.) I see Miss Brown, a teacher, walking in the opposite direction, and it strikes me it must be nine o'clock and unless we hurry we shall be late. (Miss Brown was a teacher the very sight of whom gave rise to a certain unease, if not dread, in most boys.) I ask May to hurry up, but she lags behind. It's a pity, I think, to be late on what I now take to be the very last day. (During the dream I could recall the strange sense of excitement, touched with one of loss, associated with my final day at school.) I go into the school, through various rooms full of young scholars, looking for my own classroom in the rather strange surroundings, thinking to myself, since I have been to half-past-six Mass and Communion this very morning I could always use that as an excuse for being late. (On occasion as a schoolboy

I used this as an excuse.) I make my way to the top room in the school, but when I enter it I find it is not the usual room, as big as that was, but a magnificent church, with an enormously high ceiling, a main altar and various side altars, the place crowded, every face and figure seeming unusually vivid. It is a radiant sight, bringing to mind the wonder and elation I felt on my first memorable visit to St Peter's in Rome. I stand there for moments taking it all in, see the tall figure of a priest at a side altar, intoning the Latin Mass. At this moment it seems that my mind makes a shift to a clear and elevated pitch, as I become intensely aware of the dream atmosphere of the dream, with its luminous glow, and the thought strikes me, *This is a dream, it can only be a dream, a lucid dream – one which I now remember I have had before.*

The clarity of mind instils confidence, making me feel detached and somehow above all the happenings around me. Since it is only a dream, I reason, and I know it to be a dream, something happening in my mind as I lie safely in my bed at home, there is nothing to fear, nothing to worry about, just take things as they come, for if you don't like it you can always waken yourself up. Yet as the dream proceeds, this temerity begins to dwindle away as I become aware of the dream grip upon me, and detect some cautionary hint of not being as free as I imagined. I keep trying to *think* myself out of the dream, if only for a moment, so that I shall get the sense of my being in bed, but somehow I can't make the switch. I try to reassure myself that so long as I can *think* the dream power can't have a total hold on me. And yet this trancelike feeling of being captive persists, and I have an unnerving sense of some unrevealed power, held threateningly in reserve, should I prove difficult. I turn towards the altar, from where I can hear the full-toned voice of the priest, his back to the congregation, as he solemnly celebrates Holy Mass. How wonderful it all seems, I think, how real and moving – and yet I know that in reality I am just an old man lying in bed, and all this lambent spectacle is only an illusion. But what am I to do to prove that and break free?

The thought crosses my mind that there is a perfectly simple way to prove it – since all I need to do is take a hold of the priest's vestments and give a pull. I know for certain he isn't real, and they can't be real, so that my hand will simply clutch on to thin air. And then I'll wake up – which is what I now feel I want more than anything. So I slowly approach the altar, go close up to the priest who has his big broad back towards me, at the same time telling myself that he isn't a priest at all, but just an image in my mind. Even so, I don't like taking such a liberty, not in the middle of Mass; but overcoming my reluctance – and what I sense to be my better judgement – I take hold of the tail of his chasuble. Strange, but the cloth feels real enough – as real as can be. But I tell myself that it cannot be real – and with that I give the garment a sharp tug. At once the priest turns on me, gives me such a glare of disgust and anger that I am struck with panic. Like some mad fool I have mistaken this powerful man for a dream image, and actually tugged at his vestments during Holy Mass! I must have been off my head – what made me do it! Now he makes a fierce grab, takes me by both wrists, and this move gives me an awful fright, as I feel myself in the clutch of his strong hands. I realise I have blundered unforgivably, against him and the Holy Church he represents. I cannot escape from the dream, nor can I from his most painful grip on my wrists. Have I committed a sacrilege! 'Oh God! God! God!' I cry out in despair, 'God help me!' And with one wild and desperate effort I finally break free.

The dream vanishes as I wake up and realise that I am in bed in my own bedroom. Oh what a wonderful sense of relief! I am safe – away from it all! But my wrists are painfully cramped, and I have to rub them hard to ease the stiff numbness. Once I might have imagined it was from the grasp of those powerful hands – but now I know better. The priest was only an image put on to act out a reason for the cramp – how helpless I should have been had I slept on and become paralysed! Yet so vivid was his presence that it persists in my imagination, and so I get out of bed, stretch, walk around, and write it all down. Then as it is almost time for rising I decide to have my shower – a tepid one to cool down. So refreshing is it that not only does the mighty phantom vanish into nothingness as I chuckle to myself at how easily I am scared, but as I am rubbing myself down I find that I actually feel better for the encounter – it has invigorated me both in mind and body. Thank goodness that at least I have the commonsense to see that ultimately every dream is for my good. Godlike old Dream Mind, handmaid of Nature, you might terrify me at times, but I shall always be grateful for my nightly protection.

# *Commentary*

The literature on dreaming, dating back to 5000 BC, is enormous – an assortment of contrasting beliefs and a bewildering variety of dream interpretations. There is no ancient civilisation, Babylonian or Egyptian, Indian or Chinese, Greek or Roman, lacking its own distinctive mythology of the dream. These varied from divination to demonology, of dreams being the wandering of the soul during sleep, or as messages from the gods, to whom numerous temples were built, in which dream interpreters set up their offices. Visitors often slept in the temple, hoping to induce promising dreams, or a proxy was sent to dream on behalf of another. Even the most primitive societies scattered around the globe, each established its culture in accordance with dream influences; these might decide where they lived and when they went to war, and above all dreams inspired their songs, dances, and the form of their sacrifices and religious ceremonies. It need hardly be said that the Bible, the Talmud and the Koran are permeated with revelations from dreams or visions of some kind. (All this and much more of interest can be found in *The Psychology of Dreaming* by R.L. Van de Castle.)

The only pertinent comment seems to be, and it applies

to the present-day theories of Freud and Jung, to point out once more that dreams by their very nature must accord with the dreamer's personal dream belief, and usually confirm it. Our dreams, being creations of our individual imaginations, never impose a form of imagery that would be unacceptable to us, or that we might question the reality of. If our credence weakened the dream impetus would falter – and the 'dream within a dream' subterfuge would need to come into play. This implicit correspondence between what we dream and our attitude to dreaming, means that each person's dreams are peculiar to himself alone, which in turn intensifies the hyper-reality of the dream; should the dreamer in post-sleep reflection search for a meaning in his dreams, he will always find a hint of some enigmatic truth – which on occasion proves to be correct. That is probably the reason why almost no Freudian or Jungian switches over to the rival persuasion – the same being true of most religious faiths.

Certain terrifying imagery, often of some alarming portent – the more striking the message the more gripping the dream – may leave an aftermath of apprehension in the dreamer, and in such cases psychotherapy can prove invaluable. Even the very recounting of such dream experience to an analyst may of itself prove a liberating catharsis. It took me many years to discover the blessing in disguise of so many of my own troubled dreams. Despite the hypnotic grip of the nightmare, I have finally disciplined myself to get out of bed at once on awaking to shut out all thought of the dream experience by becoming physically active, possibly sponging my head with cold water, then going off to make tea. Once the dream experience has been banished from mind, I always feel better for that seemingly wild and uncontrollable burst of fantasy. It is as though the imagination has been stimulated, so that when I sit down to work there is a certain vibrancy, a feeling of mental well-being, and the writing flows along, far better than after a peaceful sleep.

As for diagnostic hints in dreams, out of many of my own such dreams I shall instance two that were linked – one of a physical, and the other a psychic, stimulus. The first occurred in the final episode of a pleasant dream of strolling around London with a good friend, when for no apparent reason he suggested we have a wrestle in the street. (This, by the way, is an example of a dream divergence to absorb a stimulus.) At once I got my favourite grip on him, his head locked against my right hip, expecting him to submit, but to my surprise he gripped me around the middle, 'Now I'll put a grip on you!' he said, and squeezed so tightly that I felt myself blacking out. 'You win!' I cried, but he went on and it seemed my heart stopped, and as he released me I woke up to feel a prolonged 'missed heart beat' – a cardiac irregularity to which I was subject. Two weeks later, after a long day's work in the garden, I suffered a heart attack during the night. (The incipient symptom of a malfunction often goes unnoticed during the day – perhaps we shut the mind against it – but during sleep the dream must stimulate it, and usually does so in a dramatic fashion. This aspect of dreaming, I might mention, had been observed by Hippocrates in the fourteenth century BC.)

I got home from hospital feeling weak and helpless, my

mind so sluggish and disoriented that I felt I would never finish the autobiographical book I was working on. Then I had the following dream: I am myself, but as a young boy, and am walking up a cliff path, on my left is a sheer fall down to the sea, on my right a steep cliffside, the path going upwards. I meet groups of people coming along towards me, and full of self-pity I appeal to them, tell them that I am lost, and ask for their help. They each one, men and women, in turn show a detached sympathy for my plight, but tell me that they can be of no help, because in this life, they explain, each one of us has to make his way alone. No other person can show us the way. After a number of refusals, my tears and pleading having no effect, I find there is nothing for it but to set off alone along the upward path.

When I woke up I found that the dream had made such an impression on me that I resolved that the only possible way to get on with my writing was to cut out all reading, avoid abandoning my mind to any news in the media, and devote such mental powers as I might have to working on the book. This resulted in many hours of just lying down with an empty mind, not bored but longing for a read, and itching to hear some news of what was happening around the world. To satisfy this end I let my wife tell me the BBC news headlines, but I never listened to any programme, not even music. Soon I got used to this form of thought, and with my notebook handy beside me I would rest silently in the evenings, escaping the irritation that certain broadcasters, politicians especially, often aroused in me. In between I had the occasional good working day, and to my surprise I found I had the book as good as finished. (For anyone suffering from 'writer's block' I can warmly recommend it – although it demands much discipline.)

There is an ever-increasing flow of books devoted to dreaming – most attempting to put forward a rehashed viewpoint on the flimsiest speculation. The endless variety of oneirocriticism may be seen as an aspect of the human imagination in its various phases, but dream interpretation that passes itself off as a science is something quite different. Assuming a specious logicality, it can exercise that peculiar fascination of the esoteric which may impress itself on even the most rational mind, in the manner of religious indoctrination, becoming impervious to reason.

Such discrepant mythology and contrasting theories of interpretation have resulted in all dream investigation becoming controversial and suspect, with sleep research bogged down in a patchwork of contrasting theories. A clearer picture is struck when we view these dual phenomena in the context of the full day, a single twenty-four-hour rotation of the earth's axis, comprising day and night. The alternate phases of wakefulness and sleep appear antithetic, but as the unceasing neuronal activity is maintained during sleep, they are in essence complementary aspects of the vicissitudes of our solar day. During sleep the continuous current of thought, fancies, impressions and sensations is channelled into a lifelike simulation of conscious experience, mainly of a pictorial character. As we are at rest during sleep, and the happenings are purely imaginary, a situation is set up which involves the dreamer and engages his imagination, and proceeds in what appears to be a story-form sequence; waking life mentation, with thought flitting from one subject to another, could not maintain the dream flow. (The faculty of imagination would appear to serve no other biological function that that of dreaming; I suspect that all myth, story, drama and fiction originated in the dream.)

To keep its grip on the dreamer's imagination the Dream Mind will seize upon any recent thought or fancy, or a snippet of memory from years back. Unexpressed feelings are quick to surface in dreaming, especially those of guilt, jealousy, resentment, dislike or simple irritation – any that have had to be kept to oneself. In dreams they are often given a shape almost beyond recognition of the occasion that gave rise to them, the peccadillo magnified to a crime, the smothered erotic fancy to a lascivious episode – so extravagant are the dream transformations of such emotive fragments that no number of illustrations could do justice to their ingenuity. The percipient mind will often spot the sources from which they arise. The functions of dreaming are various, among which are the initiating and preserving of sleep, and the arousal mechanism by shock at any crucial moment when the sleeper would be safer awake. That a faint gleam of dream consciousness has been sustained ensures that the senses are in some state of alertness, and the dreamer is prepared for the demands of wakefulness and action of some sort. This simple psycho-physiological explanation of dreaming seems to be more in line with how Nature functions than all mythology and interpretation of the past and present – as interesting as it may be.

The literature on sleep does not compare with that of dreaming, of course, although Kleitman's bibliography of *Sleep and Wakefulness* has 4,337 references. Sleep deprivation was used by Kleitman and other investigators as a means of determining the likely functional purposes of sleep. The subjects, mainly male students, were kept awake for sixty hours or more, whilst a watch was kept on their behaviour and reactions. I shall keep to those pertaining to dreaming, and point out what I consider to be mistaken inferences that were made. Hallucinations or what Kleitman called 'semi-dreaming' occurred when the subjects were active on their feet. Towards the end of the period they could hardly keep awake sitting down, and if allowed to lie down fell asleep in under a minute. This would confirm my belief that recumbency initiates the hallucinatory phase occurring before sleep. I would also assume the hallucinations not to be a sign of diminishing mental faculties so much as a positive attempt to establish dreaming and procure sleep. Moreover, Kleitman and other sleep researchers, being unaware of the synchronised nature of dreaming and sleep – Kleitman devotes only one twentieth of his survey to dreaming – inferred that the hypnagogic phase which precedes sleep must be the prelude to it. I would differentiate, and propose that the hypnagogic hallucinations, indicating certain psychological shifts, are the phenomena that usher in actual dreaming. Yawning, stretching, drowsiness and a heavy-eyed feeling are the physical indicators of a preparedness for sleep. It is at the juncture where these dual phenomena become fused into one indivisible state, that true sleep begins. This unperceived function of the dream in safeguarding sleep is probably the main reason why there has been so little advance made in sleep research.

The initiatory phase of dreaming appears to have gone entirely recognised, and surprisingly, but logically enough, it begins the moment we lie down. I would suggest that any reader who doubts this or would care to test it, need only stand up, walk around, and at the same time observe his or her particular vein of thought and mood; next lie down supine on the floor, and gaze up at the ceiling. At once thought becomes introverted, and concentration difficult – this is even more apparent should we lie prone, face downwards. Next, cup the palms of the hands over closed eyes, when the darkness will intensify the mood to one of reverie – the ideal state to launch into dreaming and sleep. Nietzsche noted that our mental processes are conditioned by posture: 'Never give credence to a thought conceived while sitting,' he wrote – meaning, I take it, that worthwhile ideas only come when you are on your feet. (Violence at football matches, by the way, always occurs among the spectators standing on the terraces, there is no rowdiness where they are seated. Incidentally, anyone who sits down at a drinks party is likely to feel left out of it – animated conversation demands people to be on their feet. Conversely, for successful psychotherapy the couch is essential, introversion does not respond to the standing posture.)

The most striking ingenuity of the dream function is in the presentation to the sleeper of what is a spectacular flow of imagery in which he or she is involved to a varying degree, one of a sequential order, alive with action and sensation, dialogue and reflection, and always the vigilant arousal mechanism on hand should there be need for it. This apparent demythologising of dreaming must surely enhance our understanding of its inestimable influence on mankind. We dream in the womb, we dream two thirds of our time in early infancy, we dream around one third of our life from then on until death. Dreaming, I am convinced, gave birth to the human imagination. No religion, no culture, no art, that has not been inspired by the dream. If dreaming were absent from our lives there would be no music, no dance, no poetry, no literature, no civilisation (and, I suppose it would be said, no nuclear threat).

While it is not for an amateur dream researcher to make predictions – it was by pure serendipity I alighted on this discovery, a sort of reward to an assiduous and disinterested dream recorder – I am confident that sooner or later it will be substantial in sleep clinics, and should provide further insights for minds better informed than my own. What fails to inspire me is the arm's-length form of most investigation, with numerous researchers watching others dream, and so few prepared to go to bed nightly *to be dreamed*. This not only demands an innate flair for the task, and a familiarity with one's imaginational life, but immense dedication, discipline and staying power, for it is a pursuit to which there is no end, since something new can always be discovered.

To recapitulate on certain points that have been made. First, that there can be no sleep without dreaming; a dream-like stage of fantasy, brief or protracted, which we cannot normally recall, bridges the gap between being awake and going to sleep, and serves as a preliminary phase to dreaming, which initiates sleep. It has been explained how mental activity during sleep ensures an accommodating link with the mind of the dreamer, by which device calculated reactions can be evoked.

Dreaming and sleep proceed in a state of mutual synchronism, the dream always reflecting and absorbing the often spasmodic stimuli – noises and movements – that may influence sleep. (There is a tendency for dream researchers to attribute physical symptoms such as sweating and the like, to the dream, when almost invariably dreaming is actually an attempt to give expression to such – although the nightmare may aggravate a physical condition.) Early night dreaming is usually of simple character, in accord with the light sleep; the dream increases the deeper sleep becomes. Early morning dreaming after being awake, or daytime dreaming when taking a nap, is more vivid, to compensate for the higher pitch of consciousness in the sleeper.

REM sleep and NREM sleep, said to distinguish dream sleep from non-dream sleep, are simply two aspects of dreaming – vivid dreaming and quiet dreaming respectively – the latter we can rarely recall, the former often precedes arousal. What I must emphasise are the potential risks attending heavy sleep should the subject for some reason be beyond arousal by a dream shock. (I had an acquaintance, an ex-army officer, who went home one cold night after an evening's drinking, and put his feet up on the top of a stove to warm, until his wife, an actress, should arrive. She was delayed, and reached home at midnight to find him asleep in the same position, his feet so badly scorched that he died a few days later.)

That REM sleep should have been perceived first in infants is not surprising, since they above all are in need of the heightened intensity of dreaming it signifies. Children sleep so deeply that they can sleep through all manner of sound and movement, and it is crucial that they be kept on the dream rein, as it were, to ensure swift arousal. No infant should be given a soft mattress to its cot, or be in any way buried in bedclothes that would inhibit arousal limb movements.

The 'dream within a dream' does not require the involved explanation put forward by Freud, as it is simply a device by the Dream Mind of conforming at once to the dreamer's suspension of belief in the reality of the dream happenings. This allows the dream to continue uninterrupted, but viewed as a dream rather than reality. 'Recurring dreams' are a repeat of familiar themes that have served well previously; like old movies on television, however, there is a limit to how many repeats they will survive – a good number of my own have worn out their novelty and been made redundant.

'Flying' and 'falling' dreams usually occur during a volatile period, when the imagination is at a pitch too vibrant to be controlled by normal dreaming. That being the case the sleeper will soon need to be awakened, and such dreams prepare him for arousal by a possible dream shock of hitting the ground – it may be traumatic but a soft landing is always assured. Waken a sleeping person abruptly by shaking him and he is confused and helpless.

Sexuality in dreams springs from three main sources

– sexual longing, the evocation of previously unfulfilled sexual desires, and often simply the dream response to a full bladder resulting in tumescence. In dreams the sexual partner is of no real-life significance – the same being true of all dream characters, they are purely products of the dreamer's imagination. Dreaming being amoral, any makeshift character that happens to have appeared in the dream will serve. A bad-tempered woman teacher of whom I had gone in fear as a boy, a woman lacking all feminine appeal, turned up in my dreams one night, some sixty years later. I had often dreamt of her, but on this occasion as the dream went on I found we were engaged in intimate sexual exchanges. When I woke up I had need to go to the toilet and I imagine that she had to fill the role demanded by the dream.

Guilt is a most potent activator of dreams, and as such ensures us countless hours of sound sleep – even though we may wake up troubled in mind. No civilised human being with a conscience can escape a sense of guilt, since from infancy we are made aware daily of our many imperfections, misdoings, transgressions, and sins. Of course all sense of guilt, which is a form of dream blackmail, the dreamer at the mercy of his conscience, must be flung aside once we get up, and thank goodness most of us are able to forget it all. It is clear from the swift manner our dreams evanesce that they are intended to be forgotten. Although dreams may exploit our moral sensibility they are in fact amoral – just ad hoc ploys.

I feel there is little point in continuing to expose the accretion of mythology, misapprehension, and above all, mystification, that has attached itself to dreaming. Once the concept of sleep and dreaming being immutably interdependent is grasped, the theory that such a vital function of dreaming could be of an intermittent or haphazard nature, or merely serve the somewhat trivial purposes that have been suggested, will be seen to be quite inadmissible.

A most suspicious step forward would be a crucial shift in our attitude to dreaming – especially so among those engaged in psychiatric medicine. Then the dream might be seen, not for what it so often appears to be, but for what it actually is – an essential safeguard of every sleeper, felicitous rather than ominous, a blessing from above, not a bane from below. 'For as God uses the help of our reason to illuminate us, so should we likewise turn it every way, that we may be more capable of understanding His mysteries,' wrote Francis Bacon, 'provided only that the mind be enlarged, according to its capacity, to the grandeur of the mysteries, and not the mysteries contracted to the narrowness of the mind.'

*Isle of Man 1973–1990*